The heart of Kate clear faith that tru is something we do and live and bring to pass. In these essays she shows us, with lovely humility and warmth, that the life of a Latter-day Saint should be one of abundant generosity and forgiveness, directed both to ourselves and to others. Kate worked ceaselessly to live a true life. As she invites us to watch her labor may we be inspired to seek to do the same.

—MATTHEW BOWMAN, Howard W. Hunter Chair of Mormon Studies, Claremont Graduate University

Kate is a role model, particularly for women balancing competing demands for their time and energy, for doing what they feel called to do and being creative in prioritizing.

—LAUREL THATCHER ULRICH, 300th Anniversary University Professor emerita, Harvard University

Life and beauty in the face of death. In *Both Things Are True*, Kate Holbrook offers a shockingly self-aware and urgent meditation on what it is to truly live according to faith. As we balance the endless demands on time and labor, it can be easy to leave undone work that seems most vital. Through poignant experiences, both her own and those of figures past and present, Kate demonstrates how this work can be enabled through the grace of Christ and the community of Saints.

—JONATHAN A. STAPLEY, author of *The Power of Godliness: Mormon Liturgy and Cosmology*

In these essays both Kate Holbrook's striking insights and her abundant graciousness come together in inspiring ways. Whether pricking our consciences or illuminating how a tuna-noodle casserole can be a holy offering, Kate has left a work that matters, a work that calls us to a holier way of living in faith.

—AMY HARRIS, Associate Professor of History, Brigham Young University–Provo

Throughout this book, one of Kate Holbrook's greatest strengths is on stunning display: her ability to be a human bridge. In this case, she bridges the gap between unquestioning believers and those with a more natural inclination to skepticism. As I read the interview with Kate at the beginning of this book, I found myself longing to have just one more conversation with her. But, in the essays that followed, I found that thirst quenched as I was reunited, if for only a moment, with the Kate whose work has made an indelible impression on my life—the Kate who makes even the most mundane feel magical, who helps me see history through a reasonable lens, and who leaves me on each encounter longing to be better.

—MORGAN JONES PEARSON, host of *LDS Living*'s *All In* podcast

In words that are smart, honest, and deeply generous, Kate Holbrook's essays lead us through the experiences of an extraordinary woman, one deeply shaped by the religious community that she loved so dearly. Her acute observations about the details of life, both momentous and mundane, remind us that the search for truth and the need to give and receive love are both necessary and never complete. We are always building, she advises. And what a remarkable edifice of her own faith she has left for others! She invites us as a faithful guide to glimpse the world as she saw and lived it: filled with the possibility for human care and connection and steeped in the beauty of both natural and social worlds. Kate's luminous voice will surely touch readers, just as she touched so many lives and brought life to the words of many more.

—LAURIE MAFFLY-KIPP, Archer Alexander Distinguished Professor at the John C. Danforth Center on Religion and Politics, Washington University in St. Louis

For a disciple-scholar like Kate Holbrook, speaking in the language of faith is essential and speaking in the language of scholarship is essential. Both things are true, even if few people master both skills. Kate has both gifts in abundance. Her mind integrates while so many others divide, teaching that principles that are apparently contradictory are both true. She wrestles with big questions. What does it mean to say the Church is true? How does revelation come? With vulnerable personal stories and with examples from scripture, early Church history, and modern Saints from Rwanda to Russia, Kate shares her wise, empathetic voice. Most of all, these essays share her voice of faith—of faith in Jesus Christ, of faith in the Church she loves, of faith in the stories of the past to teach and to inspire, of faith in people struggling through their own mortal experience.

—MATTHEW J. GROW, Church History Department,
The Church of Jesus Christ of Latter-day Saints

In *Both Things Are True,* Kate Holbrook speaks as a prophetess crying in the wilderness. Like Miriam, she leads a generation of believers wandering through new, unfamiliar territory. Like Deborah, she is a wise judge evaluating competing moral claims. Like Anna, she bears witness of the Messiah even when He appears in humble domestic circumstances. Like Eliza, she is a leading voice within the Church. Like all of these women, Kate is a real human with fallibilities who did her best to follow God in the time she had. *Both Things Are True* is a corrective to today's brittle ideologies and polarized perspectives, calling us to fidelity to each other and to Christ.

—MELISSA WEI-TSING INOUYE, Senior Lecturer, University of Auckland; and Historian, Church History Department,
The Church of Jesus Christ of Latter-day Saints

Kate Holbrook's collection of essays opens a window into her soul—a window that was not often transparent to others. Her personal writings expose her sacred vulnerabilities as well as her core truths. I feel as though I am better acquainted with this deep, expansive part of her after reading her private words to better understand her public work. Kate lived her religion, full of careful thought and interpretation. She expands definitions while carefully and thoughtfully working through dissonance and tension to come to her wholeness. It's an enlightening view.

—JENNIFER REEDER, nineteenth-century women's history specialist, Church History Department, The Church of Jesus Christ of Latter-day Saints

Both Things Are True is a gift to those who already love Kate Holbrook and to those who will come to love her through this book. As an expert in women's history at the Church History Department, she helped expand awareness of Latter-day Saint women's contributions and the use of their words in Church settings. Her long battle with cancer focused her piercing intellect and generous spirit on important questions about life and legacy. In these essays, Kate grapples with the challenges of balancing work and home, finding belonging, and navigating thorny issues in Church history. She describes writing history as a sacred act, as weighted with the obligation to love and forgive as are our relationships with the living. Her words reverberate with her deep love for the Savior, the gospel, the Church, and the imperfect people within and outside it.

—JENNY HALE PULSIPHER, Professor of History, Brigham Young University–Provo

BOTH THINGS
ARE TRUE

A Living Faith Book

Living Faith books are for readers who cherish the life of the mind and the things of the Spirit. Each title offers an example of faith in search of understanding, the unique voice of a practicing scholar who has cultivated a believing heart.

Samuel M. Brown, *First Principles and Ordinances: The Fourth Article of Faith in Light of the Temple*

Samuel M. Brown, *Where the Soul Hungers: One Doctor's Journey from Atheism to Faith*

James E. Faulconer, *Thinking Otherwise: Theological Explorations of Joseph Smith's Revelations*

Terryl L. Givens, *The Doors of Faith*

George B. Handley, *The Hope of Nature: Our Care for God's Creation*

George B. Handley, *If Truth Were a Child*

Ashley Mae Hoiland, *One Hundred Birds Taught Me to Fly: The Art of Seeking God*

Charles Shirō Inouye, *Zion Earth Zen Sky*

Melissa Wei-Tsing Inouye, *Crossings: A Bald Asian American Latter-day Saint Woman Scholar's Ventures through Life, Death, Cancer & Motherhood (Not Necessarily in That Order)*

Melissa Wei-Tsing Inouye and Kate Holbrook, eds., *Every Needful Thing: Essays on the Life of the Mind and the Heart*

Patrick Q. Mason, *Planted: Belief and Belonging in an Age of Doubt*

Patrick Q. Mason and J. David Pulsipher, *Proclaim Peace: The Restoration's Answer to an Age of Conflict*

Adam S. Miller, *Letters to a Young Mormon* (2nd ed.)

Steven L. Peck, *Evolving Faith: Wanderings of a Mormon Biologist*

Thomas F. Rogers, *Let Your Hearts and Minds Expand: Reflections on Faith, Reason, Charity, and Beauty*

Matthew Wickman, *Life to the Whole Being: The Spiritual Memoir of a Literature Professor*

BOTH THINGS ARE TRUE

by
Kate Holbrook

DESERET BOOK

BYU Maxwell Institute

© 2023 by Neal A. Maxwell Institute for Religious Scholarship, Brigham Young University. All rights reserved. This book is the result of a joint publishing effort by the Neal A. Maxwell Institute for Religious Scholarship and Deseret Book Company.

Permissions. No portion of this book may be reproduced by any means or process without the formal written consent of the publisher. Direct all permissions requests to Permissions Manager, Neal A. Maxwell Institute for Religious Scholarship, Brigham Young University, Provo, UT 84602 or email: MIpermissions@byu.edu

The views expressed in this book are solely those of the authors and do not necessarily represent those of the editors, The Neal A. Maxwell Institute for Religious Scholarship, Brigham Young University or any of its affiliates, Deseret Book, or The Church of Jesus Christ of Latter-day Saints.

DESERET BOOK is a registered trademark of Deseret Book Company. Visit us at deseretbook.com or maxwellinstitute.byu.edu

The paper used in this publication meets the minimum requirements of the American National Standards for Information Sciences—Permanence of Paper for Printed Library Materials.
ANSI Z39.48-19

ISBN: 978-1-63993-180-4
Library of Congress Control Number: 2023904899
(CIP data on file)

Cover Design: Heather Ward
Cover Art: Courtesy of Lisa DeLong,
original artwork "Two Great Lights," 2019
Book Design: Kachergis Book Design
Printed in the United States of America

For Belle and Kathleen.
And for Amelia, Lucia, and Persephone.

CONTENTS

Prologue by Rosalynde Frandsen Welch ... ix

INTERVIEW

Deep in the Sources, an LDS Women Project Interview Produced by Nollie Haws ... 3

ESSAYS

I Belong to the True and Living Church ... 31
Revelation Is a Process ... 51
Housework Is a Crucible of Discipleship ... 75
Forgiving and Remembering ... 93
The Weight of Legacy ... 111

Epilogue by Samuel Morris Brown ... 139

Publications of Kate Holbrook ... 145
Subject Index ... 147
Scripture Index ... 151

PROLOGUE

BY ROSALYNDE FRANDSEN WELCH

"This is a collection of women speaking about themselves; their own religious thinking in their own voices." Kate Holbrook's voice came through the speaker clear as a silver bell. I was mopping the kitchen floor on a Saturday morning in July of 2022, still in the new-house phase when I thought I could keep all the things clean all the time. I'd been scrolling through old podcasts to keep me company as I worked and landed on Kate talking about a book she had edited in 2017: *At the Pulpit: 185 Years of Discourses by Latter-day Saint Women.* She had poured her heart into selecting sophisticated and diverse women's sermons, and her enthusiasm lit up my kitchen.[1]

What about Kate's own writing, Kate's own religious thinking in her own voice? The words hit me in the stomach like a gallon of PineSol. Kate had spent her entire career preserving and showcasing other women's writing. Where was Kate's own personal voice? *We need to make sure* her *writing is preserved.* The impression was urgent, an insistent companion through

---

1. "Women at the Latter-day Saint Pulpit, with Jennifer Reeder and Kate Holbrook," Maxwell Institute Podcast Episode #61, https://mi.byu.edu/mip-61-pulpit/.

the day's vacuuming and dusting. I don't think I heard another word of the podcast.

I had known Kate's work for about a decade and had collaborated with her professionally off and on over the past four years. She was a historian at the Church History Department, where she wrote about Latter-day Saint women's history. We worked together advising BYU's Maxwell Institute on its publication program. Kate had brought a quiet but steely seriousness about including women authors in the Institute's catalog. I had come to know her gentle, straightforward manner, her vision of Zion belonging, and her persistence in building that vision on careful foundations of trust.

I also knew a little bit about the eye cancer that for years had made Kate's private life a checkerboard of hope and setback. A week earlier, her husband Sam Brown had shared with friends the terrible news that her cancer had entered a terminal phase and doctors expected that she would live less than a year. I didn't quite believe it would happen so fast; I just couldn't imagine the world without Kate. Still, I thought, it was definitely time for Kate to start working on her own writing, and I knew that I needed to offer to help.

That night I wrote a careful email, feeling awkward about alluding to her cancer and sheepish for presuming that I could help.

July 9, 2022

DEAR KATE,

An insistent thought occurred to me today, to encourage you to write for and about yourself when you're able, and to offer my assistance if I can help you in any way. I feel silly offering, since writing is the last thing a person like you would need help with! But I would be honored to do anything from transcribing audio recordings or handwritten records to combining files, or any other chore that could free up your time. You spend so much time polishing and showcasing the writing of other women. It is your great gift, and what a gift to us! But the world needs your personal writing, too.

Sometimes offers of help can be a burden in themselves, because then you have to find a way to acknowledge and show appreciation for the offer! Don't let this be that! As I said, just a thought that appeared and then stayed with me this morning.

ROSALYNDE

I sent it off, still feeling the weight of the morning's impression. A few hours later, I received a reply.

ROSALYNDE,

We just tonight made a prioritized list of the personal writings that I most would like to complete, and I would be very grateful for your help. I have drafted the chapters for a Maxwell Institute book (but not yet the introduction) entitled *Two Things Are True,* and Jana Riess has edited and returned them to me. I was going to spend an hour a day next week addressing her comments, and if I could send the work I've done each week to you for whatever smoothing you were able to do, I would be exceedingly grateful. I feel that I need to just hurry and get this done as soon as I can.

Does that sound like something you might be

> able to help with? In any case, thank you so much for reaching out. Even reading your message gave me a sense of real support, both human and heavenly.
>
> KATE

Oh yes, Kate, that was something I could do, with the greatest sense of responsibility and trust I've ever felt in my professional life. Over the next month or so, Kate sent me three chapters in varying stages of completion. As her limited strength allowed, we corresponded about the work I did, tentatively at first, in drafting and editing sections of each essay. A few days before she passed away on August 20, I asked her to send me the final chapters for safekeeping. Kate's life waned much faster than I had ever imagined it would. There was just enough time for each of us to develop confidence in the process, to trust that her words could be shepherded into the book she so wanted to place in her daughters' hands.

Several women dear to Kate, fellow travelers who had known and written with her for years, collaborated in crucial ways on the development of this volume, and Sam further elaborates their contributions in the epilogue. The overarching concept of the book, as well as every chapter and every anecdote, idea, and insight, comes from Kate's mind. Our work was to smooth and expand her ideas, to integrate material from other sources of her writing when called for, and to shape each chapter to serve her vision of the fruitful tensions that enliven our journey in the gospel.

In a way, this isn't the book I would have expected from Kate. It seemed to me that Kate lived her life in a unity of faith, hope, and love. She wrote what she loved, and she wrote what she lived. She loved the domestic arts and the female conversation that filled the home she was raised in by her mother and grandmother. So, she wrote about women and their work. Kate loved creating new recipes, throwing dinner parties, and eating the best of fine cuisine or home cooking. So, she wrote about food. Kate loved the community of Saints, and she cherished the ritual power of priesthood ordinances; she revered church leadership, and she remembered our forefathers and foremothers. So, she wrote about it all. For Kate, academic history was above all a useful method to bring together everything she loved.

What I've learned is that, although she beautifully integrated her personal, professional, and faith lives, Kate was also attuned to their tensions. This, too, reflects her deep roots in our religious tradition. Joseph Smith's observation that "by proving contraries, truth is made manifest," has become a beloved aphorism of Latter-day Saint thought.[2] *Both Things Are True* is an expansion of this idea. Kate shows how a covenant life can be lived in the open space between contrary ideas that are equally valid but independently incomplete. When we learn to hold true things together in their natural tension, we find our hearts and souls stretched wide. The process can be challenging, and Kate is not afraid to explore any of it in these chapters. But the spiritual rewards are great. The prophet Enoch, when confronted with a pair of these contrary truths, "stretched forth his arms, and his heart swelled wide as eternity" (Moses 7:41).

While they originated separately, the chapters together chart a path through the heart of Kate's faith. Chapter 1, "I Belong to the True and Living Church," opens with the organizing principle of her life: her membership in The Church of Jesus Christ of Latter-day Saints. Her intellectual

---

2. "Letter to Israel Daniel Rupp, 5 June 1844," 1, josephsmithpapers.org.

gifts took her to spaces deep within and far outside the Church, and she always led with her faith. In this chapter, she explores with precision her testimony that the Church is true. What exactly do we mean when we testify, and how can we do so generously and inclusively? She returns to the Church's infancy and finds that we call ours the *true* Church because, from its beginnings, it has welcomed all truth as part of God's unfolding revelation. At the same time, the truth of our Church lies in its ongoing call for us to live in true Christlike relation to one another.

The following chapter, "Revelation Is a Process," takes the measure of the window through which truth shines into the Church. Drawing examples from Church history, Kate shows that revelation is a process like giving birth: it's often arduous and messy, it rarely proceeds according to plan, but its divine power is undeniable. Considering both personal and institutional forms of revelation, Kate finds that revelation's human dimension, amply attested in historical records, can bind us to others as we seek God's will together. Her personal knowledge of God's faithful desire to speak to his children was the bedrock of her spiritual life.

The third chapter of the book, "Housework Is a Crucible of Discipleship," may puzzle readers at first. Cleaning house, an incessant and unloved fact of ordinary life, seems out of place among the other chapters' discussions of religious truth. But Kate had a gift for drawing out the spiritual significance of human practices that other observers pass over. She applied her empathetic historian's gaze to understanding people's experience from the inside out, and to infusing the stuff of our lives, whether elevated or everyday, with value. In this unusually personal and reflective chapter, she finds that housework, no less than other daily spiritual practices like prayer and forgiveness, is an occasion to seek justice and offer mercy. Cleaning house is the concrete arena where her insights on belonging, revelation, forgiveness, and legacy become real.

Chapter 4, "Forgiving and Remembering," is the book's most pointed exploration of the idea that *both things are true*. Refusing to discount either the Christian call to forgive or the necessity for moral accountability, Kate finds a disciple's path through the tension. Drawing on scripture, history, and personal experience, she affirms that forgiveness and healing are possible in Christ. But forgiveness of evil often requires us to wisely remember, not forget, past injustices. We remember so that we can avoid repeating the mistakes of the past, collective and individual. We remember to improve, repent together, and lift one another toward Christ.

The final chapter, "The Weight of Legacy," is almost unbearably poignant to read in light of her death. Kate spent much of her life in constant awareness of its end. This awareness did not lead her to despair, but rather to sustained contemplation of her life's remnant. Her willingness to pursue this question seems to me an act of astonishing spiritual courage. She performed no false modesty: she wanted her life to be big and beautiful, a life that would endure after her death. She became convinced that enduring influence comes through the giving of the self, not its aggrandizement. Legacy is a weighty matter, but it must be held lightly.

It's worth noting that Kate thought carefully about her audience. She spent her professional life as a working historian, but she wanted this book to speak to all readers—perhaps especially those outside the world of academia and the discipline of history. Her writing is clear, inviting, and down to earth. Still, Kate's academic training comes through, especially in the way that she showcases historical events and figures. As a historian, she specialized in recovering and interpreting the voices of people whose social context was different from her own. This is the stock-in-trade of the historical method, and she worked tirelessly to do so as accurately and generously as she could. When she introduces the voices of other people in this book, she does so not to use or appropriate their perspectives for her own, but to think with them and learn from them. Likewise, Kate carefully considered how she wanted to identify the people whose voices she introduces. In the editing process, we have preserved Kate's decisions about whom to identify by first name, last name, or title.

This book holds Kate Holbrook's own religious thinking, in her own voice. It is a part of her public legacy, together with the short but significant shelf of books she edited and her many writings and recordings available online. But her legacy also lives in the bridges of understanding she built to connect Church members across the globe, brothers and sisters of different perspectives, positions, and roles. It lives in the compassionate, meticulous historical methods employed by the young historians she mentored. It lives in her recipes, her garden, her scrapbooks, and her home.

There is one passage in this book that touches me more than any other. I have returned to it again and again in the process of completing Kate's work. In chapter 2, Kate describes a green pasture high in the Uinta mountains near her family cabin. In a few simple and perfect sentences, she describes the beauty of the earth and sky she always found there, the comfort it gave her to be with the animals as they rested in the safe valley. She channels, probably unconsciously, the Hebrew poetry of the biblical prophet Joel, who similarly saw God's goodness in a scene of animals at rest:

> Do not fear, you animals of the field,
> for the pastures of the wilderness are green;
> the tree bears its fruit,
> the fig tree and vine give their full yield.
> O children of Zion, be glad
> and rejoice in the Lord your God;
> for he has given the early rain for your vindication,
> he has poured down for you abundant rain,
> the early and the later rain, as before.
> (Joel 2: 22–23, NRSV)

Kate uses the image of the still pasture, greened by early and late rains, to explain the gathering of Israel as it comes to pass in the work of the Church. But when I read it, I can't help but believe that her mountain pasture gave Kate a foretaste of her final gathering to the fold of God. She longed to be there. This book is her parting effort to help others find the way.

INTERVIEW

Kate Holbrook. <small>Photo by Samantha Kelly.</small>

DEEP IN THE SOURCES

KATE HOLBROOK

October 4, 2018
This interview was produced by Nollie Haws and originally published by The LDS Women Project[1]

As a professional historian, Kate Holbrook has focused her career on telling women's stories through the lens of two of her favorite topics: religion and food. Currently the director of women's history at the Church History Department, she talks about growing up as an only child raised by her mother and grandmother, how the Church has blessed her life from infancy, the beauty and challenges of managing a home and a career, getting rid of gospel "shoulds," and how members can constructively approach challenging topics in church history.

---

1. Kate Holbrook, "Deep in the Sources," LDS Women Project, interview produced by Nollie Haws, October 4, 2018, http://ldswomenproject.com/interview/deep-in-the-sources/. The LDS Women Project collects stories of diversity and faith from women of The Church of Jesus Christ of Latter-day Saints around the world. At the time of printing, the LDS Women Project producers had interviewed more than 250 women in more than 25 countries.

INTERVIEWER. Tell me about your upbringing.

KATE HOLBROOK. I was born in Santa Barbara, California, and my dad left six weeks to the day after I was born. The landlord decided he was going to move back into the apartment, so my mom had to move two days later with a new baby. Members in her ward just quietly came and helped her. They were packing up boxes and my mom's aunt was there, and my mom started crying. Her aunt said, "Let's take a break and come back." When they came back, the ward had finished; the apartment was completely empty. So they went to the new apartment. Her pictures were on the wall and even her toothbrush was right where it had been in the old bathroom. I've known the goodness of this Church from before I could remember.

While we lived in California, my mom taught school and I had different babysitters during the day. My grandpa died on Valentine's Day just after I turned five, and a few months later my mom called my grandma and asked, "What'd you have for dinner?" My grandma said, "A piece of candy and a Diet Coke." My mom replied, "Well, what would you think about us moving to Utah and living together?" My grandma was thrilled. We moved the summer before I started kindergarten, and my grandma took up cooking and eating meals again.

INTERVIEWER. What was your experience growing up in Utah like?

HOLBROOK. We lived in Provo, not too far away from BYU. I remember always praying when I was little that I could have a dad, that I could have siblings. But other than that, it was a really good life. My grandma was wonderful. I loved living

Kate with her mother Kathleen in Lake Oswego.

with the two of them. We had a lot of fun together. They were good at seeing the humor in things, so there was a lot of laughing. I loved to cook, and my grandma taught me how to bake. They were avid sports fans and went to BYU basketball and football games or always watched them on TV if they were away games. When I was too young to babysit myself, they would take me to the games, and I would sit there and read and the people around us would be kind of mad at me. When I was old enough to stay home alone, I would cook while they were gone to the football games and surprise them. The first time, I think I was about 10, I walked to the grocery store nearby and bought all the ingredients I needed. They came home to a three-course meal. They were shocked.

INTERVIEWER. Was there a strong focus on education in your family?

HOLBROOK. I knew there was a feeling that in our family, people go to college, and I needed to study well so I could get a scholarship. College was framed for me as, "You need to get a college degree so that if something goes wrong you can support yourself." BYU felt like the right place to go, so I did. I studied what I loved, which maybe is a little easier to do if you have the attitude that it's a backup degree, not a solid career path. I majored in English and loved it, and I was minoring in history until I served a mission in Russia. I decided to minor in Russian but found out I just needed to do a little more to make it a double major, so I ended up with degrees in English and Russian literature.

INTERVIEWER. What was it like serving a mission in Russia during the early '90s in the post-Soviet era?

HOLBROOK. It was really exciting. I was there in '93 and '94 and was called to the Moscow mission. When I arrived, they said, "We're actually sending two of you to a new mission. It's the Samara mission." They put us on a train to Samara the next day, and it felt like a tremendous adventure. I was ecstatic. I'd always been a pretty romantic young person. I had dreams of high adventure and rescuing children from burning schoolhouses, being martyred for a noble cause. So riding this train across Russia—I think a 14-hour train ride—was really thrilling. My first companion was American, and she met me at the train station. President Nelson, then Elder Nelson, was picking his son up from the mission, so I hadn't been there very long when we had a conference and got to hear him speak. That gave me the wrong impression that all these exciting things would always be happening. Because after that it was always just work.

From the time I had been there six months until the end of my mission, I was with Russian and Ukrainian companions, and that was fantastic. They were new to the Church because the Church was new in general there. I had a 42-year-old companion who hadn't been to the temple or to the MTC. She was learning what the Church was at the same time that she and I were companions, and I was half her age figuring out how to teach other people.

INTERVIEWER. What were people's attitudes toward religion in general, and Mormon[2] missionaries in specific?

HOLBROOK. Holmes' *A Study in Scarlet*. A lot of them had read that book; they're a very literate people. Much bigger readers than we are in this country. I don't know what's

---

2. This interview was conducted when "Mormon" was still a common name for members of The Church of Jesus Christ of Latter-day Saints.

happening now, but back then people would memorize poems and passages from famous books, and they really knew the Russian writers. They took the humanities more seriously there than we did at that time in this country.

People were very interested that we were Americans and a little interested in religion. But it felt so foreign to them that it wasn't something they could generally take in easily. Those people who had been religious had people in their families, often a grandmother, who secretly taught them religious sentiments. So if we came out saying something like, "This is the one true church," then it was over. They had sacrificed and risked in private, nourished this flame of belief in God, so to have us make some statement about our church being better didn't go over well.

INTERVIEWER. How did you decide you would go to Harvard and what you would study?

HOLBROOK. I was going to a PhD program in Madison, Wisconsin, in Russian literature, and a friend who was also looking at PhD programs said, "What made a big difference in helping me make my decision was to actually visit the places."

I thought maybe I should go there. I went and it just felt so wrong. There was no question this was not the right choice. It was a bummer because I had applied and been accepted, and this was a great program that I had been excited about. I got home from that trip, and I thought, "Well, I spent one rainy afternoon in Boston and fell head over heels for it. I'm just going to move there and figure out from there what I want to do with my life." So I did.

I graduated from BYU in August, and a week or two later got on the plane and moved to Boston. I went to a temp

Kate and her husband Samuel Brown. <small>Photo by Samantha Kelly.</small>

agency and got some work, which gave me the chance to try out a few different things. But really what I had in mind was working at a university so I could take some classes and figure out what I did want to do the next degree in. I ended up getting a full-time job at Boston University in their Core Curriculum program, which is a great books program, and it was like finishing school for me. The faculty members I worked with were fantastic. I got to see how people in the academy outside of BYU think and how they socialize and what they talk about. It was a really great job. I promised them I would stay for two years, and it was two years to the day. During that period of exploration, I figured out I wanted to go to divinity school and the semester started right when my two-year promise was up.

INTERVIEWER. At what point did you meet your husband?

HOLBROOK. I met Sam at a party just two days after moving to Boston. He heard me say that I spoke Russian, then at Church on Sunday, he introduced himself. I had been watching him all through Church and listening to the comments he made and was really intrigued by him. He had decided he wasn't going to date for a while, so we hung out for a couple of months. We dated for about a year and a half and then got married. I started divinity school just a few months after I got married.

INTERVIEWER. You've studied religion, gender, and food. How did those things become the focus of your research?

HOLBROOK. At Harvard Divinity School you can take courses all over the university, so I explored. I had a professor that I really liked in the divinity school who taught on religion and society, who invited me to teach with him.

I loved teaching so much that I realized I actually did want to get a PhD. I had been a little hesitant about that because I had heard such horror stories about what it could be like.

I was also trying to have a child at the time, and it wasn't working out; I kept having miscarriages. It was when I was accepted into the program at Boston University in Religion and Literature that I also had a viable pregnancy. They held my spot for me for a year, so my daughter was 11 months old when I finally started. I also kept teaching the religion class with the professor at Harvard when she was young. I would take her to lectures with me and she was really good, so we would just bring her in the stroller. If I had to participate in a lecture, one of the other teaching fellows would watch over her.

As I was deciding on a dissertation topic, I thought, "What are the things I've felt really intrigued and passionate about my whole life?" I eventually figured out that I would do a dissertation about religion and food, so automatically women's stories would be prominent in that topic. Really, it was about the everyday experience of lived religion. One chapter is just on favorite recipes, why they were embraced by the community. I read them closely, almost like you would a poem. What do we learn from the way this recipe is described? I finished my coursework when we decided to move to Utah.

INTERVIEWER. What influenced your decision to move?

HOLBROOK. The East Coast lifestyle can take a toll on family life, minds, and well-being. Even though it's such a stimulating, wonderful place to be, we wanted our family to have a little bit of a different experience. Since we were from the West, there was part of us that was deeply Western, and we valued what that had brought to our lives and wanted our children to have a similar opportunity. Especially just living around mountains and having experiences in mountains during their formative years. Of course, there are mountains in the East, but we were thinking about the Wasatch and Uinta mountains. I feel like Russia is a home to me, and I certainly feel like Boston is a home to me, so it was not a rejection of those places. But there was something about Western U.S. culture that I missed that feels like home to me.

I hoped we would feel as comfortable at Church in Utah as we did in our Cambridge ward. Then we moved here, and I thought, "Wow, was I a snob." I felt bad that I had those apprehensions about culture and homogeneity as I settled in. We've lived in two different houses here in two different wards, and just loved, loved them both. We've been lucky to be able to have those be our Church experiences here, although I don't want to say they're rare. We've been accepted for who we are. I feel like people embrace what we have to give and forgive whatever makes us weird outliers. The Church has been a really beautiful experience for both of us here.

INTERVIEWER. How did you end up at the Church History Department?

HOLBROOK. I would work half days with my little kids. I passed my oral exams, and then wrote my dissertation prospectus. While I was writing the prospectus, I read a great book that all graduate students should read called *How to Write Your Dissertation in 15 Minutes Per Day*. It's a lame title but a really useful book. The author talks about the importance of having a writing group for deadlines, support, and feedback. I put together a writing group, and Jill Mulvay Derr (a historian in the Church History Department) was

Kate in Millcreek Canyon, Utah.

in my writing group. One day she said, "I am going to retire, and they are going to replace me with somebody in a position that's specifically to study women's history." When she said that I thought, "There's my next step." I hadn't finished my dissertation yet, but it felt so right that I applied anyway.

INTERVIEWER. What was happening with women's history up until you arrived?

HOLBROOK. Jill and other female historians had done a lot over the years here with (former Church Historian) Leonard Arrington, whom they loved, who was a great supporter of women's history. When I came on, Jill was working to finish a book that she and Carol Madsen had first thought of in the year 2000—a documentary history of the first fifty years of Relief Society using documents that told that story in a vibrant way. That was the project that I inherited and got to work on as my first project here and it was published in 2016.

INTERVIEWER. What is the primary source material that you work from?

HOLBROOK. The Church archives are tremendous. They have a lot of global history too, and they're getting more all the time. The global history is just taking off here in exciting ways. Jill and Carol had already chosen—from their decades of studying Latter-day Saint women—most of the documents that would be in that book. We used other things like Relief Society minute books and other primary sources to help annotate those documents and write introductions to each one to help readers put them in context and understand their significance. Jill and I overlapped for my first few months, which was great. During that time, we had a conversation in which one of us said we really need a women's journal of discourses. From that conversation, I walked away thinking, "That's the next project." When we finished *The First Fifty Years of Relief Society*, I had already received all the approvals for us to get going on *At the Pulpit*. It was just the right book for the right time, and everybody saw that.

I think there was already a good awareness that the history needed to be more inclusive of women's experience. In some ways, five years earlier it would have been great

Kate Holbrook. *Photo by Saydi Shumway.*

to have *At the Pulpit* out, but something about the timing made it so that really everybody was ready for it. This isn't a book that only the feminists were cheering, or only the conservative people were cheering. This book crosses all those lines; it speaks to everybody. I think that's why it's part of our Gospel Library app, and now it's available in Spanish and Portuguese.

INTERVIEWER. What drives you to do history on Mormon women?

HOLBROOK. There's so much more to understand about Latter-day Saint women, and so much more to understand about the history of the Church by bringing women's experiences into it in a more vibrant way. I feel like there's a lot still to do in that area. Especially looking a little more at race and looking more globally. Sometimes those categories overlap, and sometimes they don't. I try to be cognizant that there's a lot to do in the U.S. history of the Church that's more attentive to race and also really cognizant that I'm a white person. I try to figure out how to best tell those stories from a fair and useful perspective. That will require me to consult with a lot of people who don't look like I do and ask for their help.

INTERVIEWER. How do you feel like your work can help Mormon women see themselves more fully as individuals and also as an integral part of the larger church organization?

HOLBROOK. One of the things that surprised me with *The First Fifty Years of Relief Society*, which is a heavy book and a little bit on the academic side, is women in their 60s and 70s who aren't scholars, who don't tend to read history books, would stay up late into the night reading. This book shows that women have been there, shaping the Church from the beginning. For some women, it has been really important to see that. Sometimes for a younger woman it's less of a surprise. They've come of age in a different time. They've gone to college at a different time. For the younger women, it's still really important that we study the words and insights of women and understand specific contributions they have made.

I don't know why history matters so much. But I can really feel how much it matters when I learn about these women's lives—learning the details of a life, learning how she felt. One woman featured in *At the Pulpit* had seven daughters. She would edit the *Young Woman's Journal* with one hand and hold a baby with the other or hold a meeting and at the same time darn socks for her daughters. It's so meaningful to read the way women with their responsibilities have looked historically—how they have contributed broadly without neglecting at all what was going on in their own families. Maybe it's those details that make them relatable to us as readers.

INTERVIEWER. How has your research and your work influenced how you have raised your daughters and taught them what it means to be a woman, or more specifically, a Mormon woman?

HOLBROOK. My daughters treat me so well, and part of that is when I have a Church history story to tell, they don't roll their eyes. They sit up and listen and ask questions. I've loved to know these stories, to be able to share them with them. To put forth these examples of really savvy, independent, faithful women—to show my daughters that they're part of this religious context—that means so much to me.

I love this church. I love what happens in a congregation. I love how it takes care of the needs of other people. I love how it makes me grow by trying to be aware of other people's needs and help meet their needs. What it feels like to be part of a community where you're known, where you go every Sunday, where people are looking out for you, they're helping you raise your children, and you're helping with theirs. That collaboration means the world to me. And it's not just the community. It's the community with Jesus. I don't think that this community works without Heavenly Father and Jesus, and modern revelation, and scripture. I love visiting teaching and home teaching, and now ministering.

INTERVIEWER. On your website it says you write, study, and interpret history full time. How should people interpret challenging issues in Church history that they may have not known about, or that trouble them?

HOLBROOK. It's different of course for somebody who has a PhD or is trained to interpret history, and somebody who's an everyday member of the Church who has different skills than that. Interpreting history is what I'm devoting my professional life to. For me, that means reading primary documents, reading secondary documents, reading historical context, and trying to put that all together to try to tell the most accurate narrative that I can.

But other people can come across facts that they think they should have known that they didn't know. For some people that doesn't bother them too much, but others really have a lot of pain and dissonance over that. I think when things are framed as the Church hiding something, that doesn't sit quite right with me. I don't think that's true. The last official history of the Church had plural marriage in it; it was all in there. If somebody was interested, things weren't hidden. But I recognize at the same time that they could be going to Church every Sunday, and they could have gone to seminary and never learned that Joseph Smith had plural wives, or whatever it is that's distressing. Some things haven't been emphasized, or else there wouldn't be people who are faithful, attending members, who are surprised by something later on.

I recognize that that's really hard for people and I don't want to be dismissive at all of the pain that they experience around it. For me, the Church is this really beautiful thing, and you can sit with the discomfort until it starts to make sense to you, or you can give up all of this beauty.

Facing page: Kate with her husband and children. Photo by Samantha Kelly.

I agree with Leonard Arrington that there's nothing to be afraid of in our Church history. They were humans. To study them deeply from reliable sources can be a real source of spiritual empowerment and strength. To have a partial knowledge of a few things and to not do all of the work of really going back and looking at it in context, that can lead you astray.

If you're not bothered by it, and you're not interested in history, then God bless you. Keep doing your ministering, keep doing good work. But if you're bothered by it enough to leave, or to allow it to create a real rift between you and a sense of the Spirit in your everyday life, then I think it's incumbent on you to do some digging, and to be really smart about the sources that you're using to help form your opinions. If you're only reading things from sources that are meant to tear down, then you're going to end up in a torn-down place.

INTERVIEWER. How has your work and study of history influenced your faith?

HOLBROOK. I have a real sense that God's hand is in this work, that it matters a lot. I feel a lot of spiritual direction in the everyday work that I do, from choosing what I should write this chapter about or what the next book project should be, to knowing how I should write this paragraph in a way that is true to the people it concerns and to the time it concerns. I've had sources fall into my lap. It's a lot of hard work. I don't mean it's all given to us. But there are also a lot of tender mercies that come our way.

I am also aware of all of the work that was done for decades before I got this job as a specialist in women's history. I feel very lucky because the timing for my position was right that I, with my particular aptitudes, could step in and be ready at this time when there was a real receptivity Church-wide to publishing and hearing more about women's history. That all came together in a way that was lucky for me and has felt glorious to participate in.

INTERVIEWER. Do you feel like women's experiences in the Church are different globally than in the Intermountain West?

HOLBROOK. There's a huge difference globally. It's one of the things I've seen from watching the general authorities, and I include our women leaders in the term "general authorities." They've been aware of it for decades and are still really aware. I think sometimes our concerns or priorities on the Wasatch Front, or in the Cambridge Ward, are more about the particular kind of Latter-day Saint that looks like us. I saw on my mission how women in Russia ostensibly were more equal in some ways in the workplace, but they were still doing all of the second shift work themselves. It was culturally acceptable to have a mistress. So, in some countries, to have a husband join the Church and commit only to be with them, and to be with them forever, and to really take a direct role in helping raise children, that means a lot. I care a lot about human welfare. There are a lot of cultural traditions that get meshed together when somebody joins the Church, and it's important to take those into consideration and not have an attitude of social superiority or think that we know what's right for women in general. Because sometimes in another context, in that particular time and scenario, we might be wrong.

In the *Women and Mormonism* book, Mariama Kallon who grew up in Sierra Leone said in her country there's a saying that the woman can't walk next to a man on the street because woman was taken from Adam's ribs, she belonged behind and down.³ To join The Church of Jesus Christ of Latter-day Saints where she feels that a woman walks next to a man, that's a huge shift. One she feels really grateful for.

INTERVIEWER. How have you and your husband balanced two very busy, research-driven careers at the same time?

HOLBROOK. There are concrete strategies, and each person finds her own strategy about how to make things work. We do have the funds with us both working to have somebody clean our house once a week, and that's crucial to making things function, in part because I care a lot about order and cleanliness for my psyche. For me to not break down, I need

---

3. Kate remembers this essay by Mariama Kallon with Riley M. Lorimer, "A Mormon Woman's Journey in Sierra Leone," in *Women in Mormonism: Historical and Contemporary Perspectives*, ed. Kate Holbrook and Matthew Bowman (Salt Lake City: University of Utah, 2016), ch. 21. "As I came to know the members in my branch better, I recognized that conversion to the gospel had changed the way the men and women related to each other. In Sierra Leone, a man will often say, 'How did God create Adam? First. And then Eve. And how did he do it? He took a rib out of Adam's side, so that means the woman is always here' pointing to his side, underneath his arm, 'not here,' indicating heads at equal height. 'If he wanted you to stand side by side, he would have taken a bone from the shoulder.;' But the church taught that men and women are equal—that we are all children of God. The church's teachings on the equality of men and women improved the lives of all the members greatly. In the church in Sierra Leone, men took on family responsibilities, helped with cooking and cleaning, and took a greater role in caring for children. Women took on leadership roles in wards and branches, and they were treated as equal partners in families. Where I grew up, it was difficult for women to receive an education because many people think that the more educated women are, the more prideful they become. Traditional Sierra Leonean society believes that education teaches women to want to be above the men. But when I came to the LDS Church, I found a church that values education for men and women equally. I was encouraged to get as much education as I wanted. Having sacrificed so much for education in my childhood, I felt at home."

some semblance of order. We also try to get all the laundry done in one day because then there's a beginning and an end to the task and you have a six-day break from laundry. Sometimes this works and sometimes it doesn't. I read a book twenty years ago about male-female tasks and how female tasks tend to be the kind that are never ending. There are always more dirty clothes, always more dirty dishes, things that pile up. I've tried with the domestic housekeeping part of our lives to have there be beginnings and endings to tasks as much as possible. As our kids got older, we were paying a babysitter, but it was getting easier to babysit them. We started including helping with laundry as part of what it meant to be paid to babysit our children. I think it does tend to be hard to hire help for those of us raised to be self-sufficient.

In my view, there's something beautiful about being able to run a home. It requires a lot of sophistication, intellectual work in planning, and a lot of spiritual work, like forgiveness and patience. It's hard to give up any tasks, but there are some that you need to give up. There are some that one of my best friends needs to give up, and she doesn't work outside her home. There can be too much to do, whatever your circumstances. You try to figure out, "How can I adjust this a little bit so that I'm not doing it all, so that life feels generally like a good thing instead of like a battle that I'm constantly losing?"

One of my favorite things we do is I cook on Monday nights for us and one other family, my husband cooks the next night, and the next night we have leftovers. Then on Thursday, the other family cooks for us and we get leftovers from it. It's not overwhelming because we're not cooking for six families, it's just one exchange a week. I go home from work early on the day I cook so I can make a really good meal, then stay later the other days. If nothing else, if your kids don't like what you're cooking, at least your friend might. You just want to find somebody who has a similar approach to you, whatever the approach is.

INTERVIEWER. You have battled ocular cancer. How has your experience with cancer influenced your relationship with God?

HOLBROOK. It invites you to be in a place where you really say, "Thy will be done." There's only so much you can do. You can get treated, you can try to find a doctor who is knowledgeable about whatever your issue is, you can show up, you can do the things you're supposed to do, you can suffer through the treatments. But there's a lot that you have no control over. For me, it makes the things in my life that are beautiful more poignantly beautiful, and it gives perspective. I don't know how long the good things that I enjoy are going to be around. I'm grateful for the good things, like going for a picnic with my family, and I'm going to try to make space in my life for the good things instead of putting them off. A couple of years ago, we finally got so that we were regularly doing family scripture study. It's turned into this sweet experience. If somebody's in a snit and doesn't want to join, we just do it without them. But for the people who want to come, often we just read a few verses and say a prayer and we're done. Other times people will come hang around and teenagers will start to open up and say a little about their day. We end up having this little extra time together that feels like a gift.

INTERVIEWER. So much of your professional and mental energy is taken up with Church stuff. How do you approach scriptures as personal devotion?

Kate and her husband Samuel Brown. Photo by Saydi Shumway.

HOLBROOK. I had a dentist 20 years ago who was trying to get me to floss, and he said, "If right now you're flossing once every two months, then see if you could bring it to once every two weeks." I thought that was a really good way to think about Church stuff too. That flossing conversation made it so I started reading scriptures on my own daily. I worked into it gently once a week, and then a little more, and a little more.

I think it's good to get rid of "shoulds" or some ideal sense of "this is what scripture study looks like." Follow your bliss in scripture study. They are a gift to us. If you're wondering, "I always hear about Ammon, and I kind of forget who he is except for this one thing," then maybe you want to spend a week reading the Topical Guide entries about Ammon. Or if there's a story that strikes you, maybe it's a parable in the New Testament that's hard for you to get your head around, that's a good sign. I think discomfort means there's something that's not obvious to me here. There might be a big payoff if I spend some time with it.

Spend the time—prayer time, staring into space time, reading time. I don't mean you need to study scriptures for half an hour a day if that doesn't fit into your life. Just five minutes a day. Let yourself be free to treat these as a gift instead of as a duty. Maybe there are ways that apply to your relationship with Church history, too. The people who study the men's version of Church history, there are facts that they will have at their fingertips that I do not have. I've thought, "Well, a lot of people know those things really well. I'm going to focus my energy on the things that people don't know, and things that might still be buried in this library where I work." I don't feel guilty about that. I feel I'm focusing on this thing that I was put on the earth to learn and to give. I think for an everyday person, who is not a historian, you can approach Church history that way too. "I want to learn more about this woman." "I wonder what it was like at this time." Just read up on *that*.

I love it when I have a teaching calling; it gives my study direction. Right now, I'm a gospel doctrine teacher in my ward along with my husband. I teach every other week and always have in my mind, "What's the next lesson?" I do this even on weeks when I'm not teaching; I'll read the scriptures we're going to be talking about over and over and really try to let them sink in. I like to read *The Jewish Study Bible* from Oxford. It's really helpful from the perspective of a Church member wanting to study her scriptures because the commentary is reliable and the translation is more clear than the King James translation. This translation helps me to love what I read in the Hebrew Bible.

I do want to give a plug here for *Saints*, the new Church history. The day it was released in English, it was released in 14 different languages. The way they have incorporated women's experiences and contributions works well. I love that it's written in an accessible way. I love fiction and *Saints* feels more like entering a world where physical sensations are described and there's dialogue. The thing that's great, and it was super labor intensive, is that all of it is accurate. If it says it was an "extra hot summer," they've done that research. And all those things we were talking about, the facts people thought that they should have known but didn't, they're in this book. Plural marriage is in the book, the seer stone, the Urim and Thummim. *Saints* is really a resource book, not just a history book to put on your shelf. This can be your way to engage with Church history.

AT A GLANCE

Name: Kate Holbrook
Age at Time of Interview: 46
Location: Salt Lake City, Utah
Marital History: Married to Samuel Brown since 1998
Children: 3 children
Occupation: Historian
Schools Attended: Brigham Young University, Harvard Divinity School, Boston University
Favorite Hymns: "Come Thou Fount of Every Blessing," "Lead Kindly Light" and "For the Beauty of the Earth"
Website: www.kateholbrook.org, https://www.theawaycafe.com/

ESSAYS

I BELONG TO THE TRUE AND LIVING CHURCH

Just before leaving for her first year at Cornell University, a young friend of mine approached me with a question on her mind. She had been a Church member for a little under two years, and she wondered about the teaching that the Church is true. It's a claim so familiar that many of us take it for granted: ours is "the only true and living church upon the face of the whole earth" (D&C 1:30). When she was baptized, my friend had accepted membership into the Church and entered a covenant relationship with God and her fellow members. But she still wasn't sure how to explain to classmates what it meant to say that the Church is "the only true church." She wasn't even sure why the concept of an "only true church" was necessary.

Her question got me thinking. It's an excellent question, and she's far from alone in asking it. What does it mean to say that this is the "true church," if other religious groups also influence their members to lead good lives and help them feel close to God? What does it mean to say that this is the "true church," if our historical records reveal a sometimes-messy process of God working with fallible humans? I'm not going to do justice to that question in this short chapter. Let's just be clear about that. But I do hope to share some ways of thinking about the truth that is in our Church—and the truth that we can make in and of our Church.

The discomfort that prompted my friend's question arose, I believe, because the "only true church" claim at times does not feel loving. It can feel exclusive, as if we're discounting the value of other faith traditions, or arrogantly boasting in ourselves. While some of us find the security of belonging to the one true Church appealing, for others of us it creates substantial psychological dissonance between our devotion to our own faith and our appreciation of other churches and other sources of truth. We see and celebrate the fact that other religious groups provide benefits to their own members, consistent with God's universal mercy. We don't want to discount those benefits. We don't want to be arrogant. We don't want to blind ourselves to the goodness of other people, and we don't want them to feel that we don't see their goodness. So, what does it mean to say that the Church is true?

Let me be clear. I don't just study this Church, I live it. And I love it. I've raised my children in this Church, as my own mother raised me. Mothers are famous for making lists—packing lists, chore charts, grocery lists. I have a list of my own: a list of reasons why I love this Church. These are practices and doctrines so dear to me that I could never leave. Here are a few of them:

- Children under age eight are assured salvation through Christ's grace.
- Post-mortal preaching in the spirit world gives all people a further opportunity to find God.
- We are connected to our ancestors: we take care of them, and they take care of us.

- Jesus performed the atonement to save us in His love.
- The Book of Mormon, including the sermon of King Benjamin, teaches us how to develop charity and reveals Christ as merciful and involved in human history.
- We are supported and needed by a ward family.
- Rotating leadership puts us on equal footing and allows us to share burdens.
- The Restoration gives us a generous vision of redemption.
- The Church instructs us on being good citizens.
- In church we learn reliable temporal principles and habits that promote happiness on earth.
- We enjoy the freedom to interpret the gospel according to our conscience.
- We are connected to one another through the ministering program.
- We know our Heavenly Mother.
- We benefit from the wisdom of our women leaders.
- We are enfolded in a familial relationship with Jesus and God.
- We support one another to foster emotional and physical health.
- Men cry often and without shame in church.
- Babies to play with are abundant.
- We are taught about the power of personal revelation.
- The welfare program cares for the most vulnerable among us.
- Latter-day Saint Charities perform lifesaving and life-enhancing work around the globe.
- Patriarchal blessings connect us to communities in the past and present, and orient us toward the future.

- Priesthood blessings give us direct access to the loving power of God.
- Our egalitarian teachings and communities break down caste systems.
- And finally, God needs each one of us—we're each crucial to building the kingdom.

Aside from all these reasons, however, I have chosen to live my life in the Church simply and finally because I believe it is true. In this chapter, I've tried to bring more precision to that belief. I've spent my career studying Church teachings and history carefully. I've compared them with other options and chosen with my eyes wide open. When I say I believe the Church is true, I mean that I believe God is in this Church, and that both the leaders and members receive true inspiration from God according to their stewardships. I believe that the true power of God, which we call the priesthood, is in this Church. I've felt it, I've seen it, and my professional life immerses me in sources that reinforce it. My Church life reinforces it. My family life, which I hold particularly dear, reinforces it.

When it comes to the Church, both things are true. The Church is true because it contains eternal truths and saving priesthood power and ordinances, and because it teaches its members to seek and embrace all truth. At the same time, as Elder Uchtdorf taught us, "the Restoration is an ongoing process."[1] This is part of what it means that our Church is "true and living": the Church is always *becoming* true as it grows and adapts to new circumstances and challenges. One of the

---

1. Dieter F. Uchtdorf, "Are You Sleeping through the Restoration," *Ensign*, Apr. 2014, 59. https://www.churchofjesuschrist.org/study/general-conference/2014/04/are-you-sleeping-through-the-restoration?lang=eng).

ways the Church becomes true is through our own efforts to build it truly. The truth of the Church must be constantly replenished by the faith, hope, and charity of its members. When we build Christlike relationships with one another, we make the Church true.

The True Church: Seek and Embrace All Truth

As a graduate student, I studied the history of Latter-day Saint foodways, the academic term for a people's eating habits and cooking practices. From the beginning, our foodways revealed the priority our people placed on the virtue of self-sufficiency. During the Latter-day Saints' first years in the Salt Lake Valley, Brigham Young worried about the reliability of a food supply that required Saints to trade with outsiders who might become hostile or mercenary. He pleaded with Church members to store grain and food for times of hardship, and in 1876 he put Emmeline B. Wells and the Relief Society in charge of grain storage. As a result, for just over a hundred years, Relief Society women worked together to raise, purchase, trade, glean, share, sell, and above all *store* wheat. The image of a wheat sheaf still appears on the Relief Society seal and the Relief Society building on Temple Square, a symbol of the hard work and resourcefulness that created abundance for all.[2] This emphasis on self-reliance was carried forward in the Church Welfare program, officially launched in 1936. The program encouraged Church members toward self-sufficiency in growing their own food, living frugally, and storing a supply of food in their own homes.

2. See Kate Holbrook, "Radical Food: Nation of Islam and Latter-day Saint Culinary Ideals (1930–1980)" (PhD diss., Boston University, 2014), 73, https://hdl.handle.net/2144/15142.

The virtue of self-sufficiency proved its worth when, for example, the Relief Society was able in 1906 to donate wheat to earthquake victims in San Francisco and to famine victims in China. The Saints not only had enough wheat—they had enough to share. A program intended to care for their own people without relying on sources outside the community ended up allowing the Saints to bless peoples beyond the borders of their mountain home.

Our history of valuing self-sufficiency may help us to understand why Church members have sometimes treated the truth of the Church as a kind of secure storehouse in which we can protect and store up the doctrines we treasure. If truth were like wheat, perhaps we would want to harvest it from our own fields, save it up to support our own people, and feel reluctant to accept it from those outside our own community. But my research into Latter-day Saint foodways revealed another dynamic in play. Even as Relief Society sisters stored wheat so that they would not have to rely on outsiders, they were influenced by communities outside their own. I loved examining the history of table settings, for example. Relief Society sisters found a path between their ethic of homespun self-sufficiency and the refinement of the elegant table settings they saw in outside communities. They responded to the beauty of a gracious table. To this day, Relief Society tables are often elegantly adorned with care and attention. In my research, I saw how sisters borrowed certain table norms from the dominant culture, practices and decorations that corresponded with their own values and sense of identity.[3] Self-sufficiency always co-existed with communal giving and receptivity.

3. Holbrook, 153.

The same is true of the truth we treasure in the Church. We cherish the exhilarating, expansive gospel precepts revealed by Joseph Smith, contained in Restoration scripture, and elaborated by God's continuing revelation to modern prophets. The restoration of priesthood, God's power on the earth, and His continuing revelation to prophets are truths worthy of celebration. Historical sources convince me that God's revelation to individuals has continued, and this restored gospel has made that experience available to people all around the globe. But the homegrown truths we cherish need not blind us to the beneficial aspects of other traditions. When Latter-day Saints are tempted to discount the value and beauty of other faiths, they ignore another of our homegrown truths, the thirteenth article of faith: "If there is anything virtuous, lovely, or of good report or praiseworthy, we seek after these things." Rather than downplaying the spiritual benefit of other churches, a more useful approach is to acknowledge God's work in many faith communities and then to magnify the goodness of the tradition we've chosen. For Latter-day Saints, that means *both* appreciating what is virtuous, lovely, and praiseworthy in other traditions, *and* really focusing on what our Church has to offer. We acknowledge the good here, and we are grateful for it. We do the valuable work to which our Church calls us. We bring the good we find elsewhere into our spiritual practice here. We add wheat to wheat, and we find that we have enough—and enough to share.

Of course, other churches are not the only sources of truth beyond our own community. Life is full of voices and agents in search of truth—scientific truth, philosophical truth, political truth, ecological and artistic and psychological truth. And often these truths compete with one another.

If you're engaged in life, if you take thinking seriously, then you're going to experience psychological dissonance. You will wonder how best to fulfill your mission on earth in the face of vast human suffering and your own limitations. You will wonder about the overwhelming question—and I'm being serious here—of what to eat for dinner in light of your budget, your health, your pleasure, your companions, climate change, and global hunger. Dissonance bubbles up through each of these issues and demands our attention.

Before we proceed, let me make something clear. You don't *have* to have questions about Church history or doctrine—or about any of the realms of truth out there. Every person will have different matters that bother them on this earth. Life is so rife with paradox that you should never feel there are certain topics you must suffer over if they don't naturally cause you suffering. Don't borrow other peoples' questions, because the questions that genuinely fascinate you will be the ones you can most fruitfully explore.

When you find that you are internally compelled to seek the truth of a difficult question, however, you will have to embark on a search. Let me give you an example. When I first started thinking about what it means that the Church is true, and what it means to reconcile the Church's truth with all truth, I remembered a quotation I once heard attributed to Brigham Young. I'd heard it as a child, and it has profoundly shaped the choices that I've made in my life and my attitude to this beautiful world and all the beautiful things that I embrace in it. But I'd never been able to find the exact quotation I once heard. This is how I remembered the gist of the passage: "There's truth everywhere and you should be open to it and look for it." I tried to track down the actual quotation and see whether I remembered it correctly.

At the Church History Department, we have an expert in shorthand, LaJean Carruth. LaJean translates Church leaders' talks from the nineteenth-century Utah period, when they were originally recorded in a special script known as Pitman shorthand. Her translations are often substantially closer to what speakers actually said than is the text published in the *Journal of Discourses*. If you appreciate the quotation I'm about to share, enjoy knowing that it was from the reliable work of LaJean Carruth, and know that you can find more of her careful work in the Church history catalog.[4] It turned out that what LaJean sent me wasn't the exact quotation that shaped my thinking long ago, but it is on the same topic. And it's likely more reliable than whatever I initially heard.

Brigham Young said, "[The Church] embraces every science upon the earth. Every knowledge that is imparted to men is from God and is within our religion. There is no truth that has ever been revealed that we do not believe and, at the same time, when people are disposed to point out errors . . . we are willing to acknowledge that we have errors."[5] What does "the true Church" seem to mean to Brigham Young in this quotation? I hear him saying that there is space in the Church for whatever genuine scientific or religious discoveries come along. There is truth everywhere, and this Church will try to function as a collection house for it all. I also hear him saying that the Church will have errors. We should be open to correction and new information. There's

---

4. LaJean Carruth, "Preached vs. Published: Shorthand Record Discrepancies," https://history.churchofjesuschrist.org/blog/preached-versus-published-part-1-of-3?lang=eng.

5. Brigham Young, 8 March 1868; transcribed from George D. Watt's shorthand record by LaJean Purcell Carruth.

real spiritual confidence in this quotation, the kind of confidence that stands behind a bold statement such as "There is a true Church, and this is it." And there's also the humility that blooms from spiritual confidence: "There's a truest Church and, even so, we bumbling humans aren't going to get everything right. Also, our members and our leaders are not going to be the sole source of truth. God will reveal truth elsewhere and we are still beholden to that truth, even though it doesn't come from us." Those sentiments feel awfully modern to me, but they coincide with what I think Brigham Young intended to convey.

Over the course of nearly two hundred years, Church leaders' feelings about the outside world have warmed and cooled. This was also an important realization during my graduate research into Latter-day Saint foodways. I found that leaders' openness to other communities waxed and waned depending on how much mainstream American society seemed to have in common with Church leaders' priorities, how threatening leaders judged dissonant voices to be, and what these leaders heard from God. Evidence from my own spiritual life has taught me that it's right to seek out and embrace wisdom beyond what the Church institution provides. The Church can't replace the academy, the art world, or the fields of science. The Church has its own mission, and in fulfilling that mission it can't fill those other realms as well.

I see support for the Church's early open attitudes from our current prophet, Russell M. Nelson. When he was president of the Quorum of the Twelve and dedicated the new BYU Life Sciences building in 2015, he said: "There is no conflict between science and religion. Conflict only arises from an incomplete knowledge of either science or religion or both.... All truth is part of the gospel of Jesus Christ. Whether truth comes from a scientific laboratory or by revelation from the Lord, it is compatible."[6] For me, there's ample evidence from Church leaders and my own experience to begin a definition of what it means that the Church is true. It means that the Church is not in competition with other seekers of truth. It means the Church has nothing to fear from outside sources of genuine truth but encourages us to embrace them. It means that the Church is true because it teaches its members to seek and incorporate all truth.

But when we seek truth widely, when we add wheat to wheat, we must be responsible in our search. Responsible seeking is something I've practiced as a historian. Note, for a moment, the process I followed to track down that quotation from Brigham Young. First, I took care to question my own memory and motives, to avoid self-deception, selfishness, or careless error. Second, I sought out the most reliable sources of information, aware that not all sources—historical or otherwise—are equally reliable. Third, I compared my finding with other reliable sources to confirm or discount its accuracy. Only then did I feel confident that I'd arrived at the truth.

When making a definitive statement about an event, a historian can't rely on a single source, even if it's a strong source such as a journal entry or newspaper article recorded right around the time the event took place. Every source has strengths and vulnerabilities, and to give a reliable accounting of them, historians must think carefully about those different aspects of the source. If possible, we find additional

---

6. Marianne Holman Prescott, "Church Leaders Gather at BYU's Life Sciences Building for Dedication," *Church News*, April 17, 2015, https://www.Churchofjesuschrist.org/Church/news/Church-leaders-gather-at-byus-life-sciences-building-for-dedication?lang=eng.

sources, preferably ones that have different strengths and weaknesses. When seeking answers to gospel questions, we should likewise seek different kinds of evidence. These could include the fruits of a practice; doctrinal statements repeated by multiple leaders in myriad contexts; reliable insights from a professional field; spiritual instincts honed through prayer, scripture study; and experience gleaned while attending church or while serving. In many cases, historical context will also be relevant. We should try to avoid self-deception and error by asking ourselves, "how solid is my evidence?" Also, "where does my evidence lead?"

Several years ago, I edited a book that gathered significant speeches by Latter-day Saint women. As I read widely in the archives, I discovered a talk given by the geologist Julie Willis, entitled "Gaining Light through Questioning." Willis describes her experience with a long search for spiritual truth. Her quest began with an impatient phase during which she demanded answers directly from God. But with time and spiritual maturity, she found that the quality of her questioning changed, and she began to find light from surprising sources around her. She writes:

> I no longer demanded an answer, and I didn't limit the timeframe, or how or where I would receive insights. The answer didn't come all at once. Insights came at odd times and in odd places: while reading an article in a non-LDS magazine, left on an airplane; evaluating a statistical analysis in a newspaper; listening to a discussion in ward council; or doing the dishes. I found it surprising that many of my insights did not come while listening to general conference or during scripture study; but when

I received an insight I could see how it fit directly with those sources.[7]

Over a period of years, Willis's question was answered line upon line. She describes the experience like a dimmer switch gradually increasing in brightness. Even when she had answered the question to her satisfaction—when she had enough light to see around the room comfortably—she continued to find new ideas that added insight. What if she had never asked the question and launched her search for truth?

The Church is true because it empowers its members to seek and find all truth that is "virtuous, lovely, of good report or praiseworthy," whatever its origin. The Church is a storehouse for truth, and its doors are propped open to give and receive all true things and to expel error. We add wheat to wheat, light to light, and we work toward the time when all will be nourished in body and mind.

The True Church Brings Us into True Relationship

Because I work at the Church History Department, people often ask me about historical issues that they and their students or children find disconcerting. Both the Church and my department put a lot of effort into helping people, both in and out of the Church, to obtain accurate, reliable information about Church history. I hope that those materials will be helpful to those of you who care about Church history. But because they are true, they are not tidy. The records

---

7. Julie Willis, "Gaining Light through Questioning," *At the Pulpit: 185 Years of Discourses by Latter-day Saint Women,* ed. Jenny Reeder and Kate Holbrook (Salt Lake City: Church Historians Press, 2017), https://www.churchhistorianspress.org/at-the-pulpit/bonus-chapters/bonus-7?lang=eng.

are true representations of a complicated world, and they can prompt further questions or concerns about our history and our faith. But I know these questions and crises are surmountable.

An aside about these concerns: one particular worry that seems to carry a lot of weight with us humans is that we might spend a life in faith and then find that one of our particular beliefs was not accurate. Many of us are scared of looking like dupes—coming to find something we believed in wasn't true. I think we would do better to worry more that we may be leading a selfish life or an angry life than by worrying that our conception of tithing or Sabbath observance is not quite accurate.

One more aside: I'm leaving that last sentence in there as a teaching moment to invite you into the process I go through when I write something that I believe but that also, at the same time, doesn't feel quite right. Here is what went on in my head. I wrote the sentence, and then I felt hesitant. I believe it, but it's also not quite fair to many people who struggle in their faith. There are some people who split hairs about the details of religious life. But far more often the people I encounter with a faith crisis wonder sincerely whether this tradition that has taught them to be loving is still the place that can most effectively cultivate their most-loving selves. They aren't worried that it will turn out they could have spent their whole lives drinking coffee. What they really worry about is whether to stick with all the beauty they see in this Church when there are also things they don't understand.

Discomfort comes up in me again as I write this. I don't want to remind you of those things, such as the temple and priesthood ban for women and men of African descent—or of ongoing conflict in the present. I believe deeply that our Church is so much more than those difficult matters, and I don't want to belabor them because I haven't figured them out. I also accept that since I am not an apostle or prophet, making Church policy statements is not my stewardship. I accept that there may be information to which I am not privy. I feel caught between competing ethical imperatives. I don't want to do harm to individuals who are struggling. I don't want to do harm to the Church. I don't want to misrepresent any side. I want to support faith and I want to be a conduit for truth. This chapter is difficult to write.

But notice what my struggle is really about: at heart, I'm divided about how to do right by my relationships with other people. My confusion is only secondarily about the Church's history or truth claims. For me, the most urgent and relevant questions about the truth of the Church have to do with our relationships to one another and to God. Do you find God in the Church? Does earnest Church participation bind you to others? Does the ritual and service you engage in at Church enlarge your soul? To prioritize the relational dimension of truth is not to discount the importance of our doctrine and history, nor to sweep any of it under the rug. It is simply to recognize that the point of Church doctrine and history has always been to create enduring relationships sealed in Christ. I believe that focusing on the truth of our relationships within the shelter of Church is the best way to demonstrate genuine fidelity to the truth of our doctrine and history.

I love the word fidelity. By *fidelity,* I mean the kind of faithfulness that spouses offer each other, a loving commitment to honor vows and be true to one another in all things. In fidelity to the Church, we commit to being in true and faithful relationship to God and to one another. Jesus talked about this in terms of fruit trees: does the tree's fruit taste good or bad (Matthew 7:15–20)? When you've spent a good long time serving others, praying, studying prophets' words, and attending church, what is the fruit in your life? When you do those things, do you feel more or less love for others? Has the time spent left you feeling hopeful or desolate? What does it look like for you to have your fruit taste good or bad? Practicing fidelity means looking for the best in each other. Fidelity is giving each other the benefit of the doubt; praying about our questions, fears, and shortcomings; and also praying for each other.

This leads me to the most important part of what I want to say about the true Church. My definition is not sealed; it's flexible and living, like the true Church itself. The Church I belong to is true because it brings me into enduring relationship with God and with people. My true Church is open to truth of many kinds from all good sources. The Church is the true Church, and it's also one of many sources of beauty, wisdom, goodness, and God. With a consummately loving, socially conscientious backbone, my Church works, through its members, to take care of everyone—poor, rich, challenged, smart, those who are innately spiritual, and those who are less so. The Lord's voice to Joseph Smith and Sidney Rigdon is His voice unto all: "Behold, I say unto you, that ye must visit the poor and the needy and administer to their relief, that they may be kept until all things may be done according to my law which ye have received" (D&C 44:6).

That last line, a nod toward the promise of a Zion community that leads our Church into the future, points to an additional layer of what it means to say this Church is true and living. I believe there is something aspirational about calling this Church true. We members have a commission to make it true. We should try to make it true by being true to one another. It will take work to be true. I believe we experience this aspirational dimension of truth in the Church when we forgive each other, are present with each other, and serve each other with fidelity. As we follow God's commandment to care for each other, our wards become true vehicles for God's love and grace, binding us to one another even more firmly.[8] The Church is true in the sense that it holds revealed truth and saving ordinances. And in another sense, in an ongoing relational sense, the Church will *become* true as we make our relationships true.

The fidelity that we practice within the Church should extend to our friends who may leave the Church, as well. My husband and I are blessed with beloved friends who grew up in the Church but stepped away as adults. They are generous and true friends. We love them unconditionally and hope that they'll always feel our love, regardless of their religious affiliation.[9] For Sam and me, our participation in the true Church gives us a true view of others, including those whose choices and experiences take a different path from ours. Our associations in Church—and continuing outside of Church, as in this case—open our minds and hearts to all of God's children by stripping away our natural self-absorption and our learned prejudice.

I'll never forget a beautiful interaction I witnessed once at church, a moment that captures what I'm saying about the true Church calling us into true relationship with each other. One Sunday, a twelve-year-old young woman in our ward sat on the stand, prepared to speak to the congregation. When

---

8. Kate Holbrook and Samuel Brown, "The Gift of Participating in Church," *Ensign,* Mar. 2020,

9. Holbrook and Brown, "The Gift of Participating in Church."

her turn came to stand at the pulpit, she shook her head to indicate that she was not ready. The next speaker stood and spoke first, but when he concluded, the congregation's attention returned to the young woman. She tearfully moved to the podium, but no words came. As the congregation sat in sympathetic concern for her distress, several members of her Young Women class spontaneously stood and walked together up the aisles to the stand. They surrounded their friend in a silent circle of friendship and strength. They touched her gently as she opened her mouth, tested her voice, and delivered her talk to the congregation. How did these true friends know how to support her? I believe that their experiences in church taught them. Because of church, they knew each other, they had practiced looking for and ministering to needs, and they had learned to give and receive service. Their covenants transformed ordinary acquaintance into a holy togetherness—into charity.[10]

Introspection and thought are necessary elements of our search for truth. So are prayer, worship, obedience, and study. In no way, however, can they replace service. The life Christ lived and the path he taught were sacraments of service. We find God, and build his true Church, in service to other people. The truth of the Church lies in the faithfulness and charity of its members. When we build true relationships with one another, we make the Church true.

I believe that both things are true: our Church is true, and it is living. It is perpetually becoming true. In this essay I've explored two of my reasons for that belief—namely, that the Church teaches its members to seek and embrace

---

10. Holbrook and Brown, "The Gift of Participating in Church."

all truth, and that it calls us into true relationships with one another.

When preparing my dissertation, I came across a story I particularly love. It combines so many of the things that light me up: traditional foods, sacred service, and sisterhood. And, of course, my Church. It's the story of a woman, Trish, who, separated from the Church for decades, eventually found herself dying from liver cancer. Cancer is a cruel thief of appetite, and the refined New England fare that Trish had favored during her adulthood held no appeal to her ravaged palate. Instead, she developed an urgent craving for the tuna noodle casserole she had known at church potlucks in her youth. And she knew how to get it: "'Call the visiting teacher,' Trish said in a whisper, 'and tell her to bring the good food with the tuna and noodles in it. Remember it?' she said, almost pleading. 'It had cream of mushroom soup and cornflakes on top.'" Trish's sister called the visiting teacher, who indeed knew how to make tuna noodle casserole and brought it over in time for dinner that night. Trish's sister later recalled, "It was exactly as Trish remembered it, and she ate with pleasure. It was what she needed most to eat before she died. My mother and I took turns feeding it to her."[11]

It's difficult to serve tuna noodle casserole elegantly on a plate. It's a bit messy, but it's nourishing, and, in this case, it was exactly what was needed. Life in a community of fallible humans striving to know God is likewise messy. Our historical records bear witness to the kind of relational truth that is both messy and nourishing, to the kind of church that is

---

11. Judith Dushku, "My Sister's Banquet," in *Saints Well-Seasoned: Musings on How Food Nourishes Us— Body, Heart, and Soul*, ed. Linda Hoffman Kimball (Salt Lake City: Deseret Book, 1998), 72–4. Quoted in Holbrook, "Radical Food: Nation of Islam and Latter-day Saint Culinary Ideals (1930–1980)," 55–6.

both true and becoming true. I want to leave you with my statement of faith: that we find God in doing good for other people. I have learned the most about Jesus when I have tried to do the work of Jesus.

The doors of our storehouse are open to give and receive truth from all corners, and to acknowledge and correct error. We add wheat to wheat. Our Church is true and living, as we are true to one another.

REVELATION IS A PROCESS

Patterns of Revelation

When Joseph Smith went to the woods to pray one spring day, he was not yet a prophet. At that point, he was a boy who read his Bible and felt eager to know God's will. Two hundred years later, we can take some important messages about personal revelation from the encounter he had that morning. One of them is that family status, education, wealth, and maturity are not the things God takes into account when deciding to communicate with us. Let's think about the beauty of this for a moment. Not only does it not matter where our parents went to college, it doesn't matter *whether* they went to college or whether they can read. And those things don't matter about you, either. Are you out of money? Not relevant. Does your home have a dirt floor? Doesn't matter. This is good news for those who throughout history had less access to institutional religious authority. For many women in the world, for example, interaction with God felt out of reach because it was associated most often with men and priestly office. But the First Vision and the Restored Gospel provide a balance to that: Joseph Smith was in his early teens when he prayed, and he wasn't ordained to any priesthood.

Instead, he was a person who learned from the scriptures and had enough faith to pray and ask for answers. His mother followed a similar pattern, and she also did not have the priesthood.[1] We can do that, too. Although we aren't called by God to restore the fullness of the gospel, God does call us and teach us how to be more effective, wise, and loving—more like our parents in heaven.[2]

Part of being human is making peace with our limited understanding, while holding faith that the light will grow. Joseph Smith told people about the godly aspects of his First Vision several times during his lifetime, and I'm grateful for that. Sometimes a historian has only one source to rely on to try to figure out what happened, but Joseph Smith gave us more than one way to understand. He described the experience differently at different times because he was in front of particular audiences and wanted to emphasize what mattered for each of those audiences—just as I tell an anecdote in one way to my adult friends, another way to my children, and still another way in Gospel Doctrine class, depending on how I understand the needs of and my goals for each audience. But I also think Joseph Smith described his sacred experience in various ways at different times because his human understanding of what happened increased over time. The more experience he had and the more skill he acquired in receiving and interpreting revelation, the more he understood what had happened that morning in the grove.

---

1. "Lucy Mack Smith, History, 1845," 49, The Joseph Smith Papers, https://www.josephsmithpapers.org/paper-summary/lucy-mack-smith-history-1845/56.

2. Dallin H. Oaks, "Apostasy and Restoration," *Ensign*, May 1995, 84, "Our theology begins with heavenly parents. Our highest aspiration is to be like them."

Just as Joseph understood his vision in different ways over time, there are multiple insights we can draw from his experience. In addition to demonstrating that you don't have to be important or successful in the world for God to talk to you, the First Vision tells us that God loves Jesus, responded to a boy's prayer, and forgave that boy's sins. But there is also a lot that the First Vision does not teach us. For example, it does not offer any guidance at all about Relief Society, priesthood power, baptism, or temple ordinances. It does not explain how often God will answer prayers or in what form. One major lesson the First Vision *does* teach about revelation is that it is not the same thing as an instruction manual. Revelation is more like a treasure map, with an X marking the treasure, a river and some trees as landmarks, but significant detail left out. Revelation can be slow, spotty, and take a while to figure out. In the words that I first heard from Sister Sharon Eubank: "Revelation is a process." I have found two things to be true about revelation, whether it comes as the personal light we receive for ourselves or the prophetic light that guides the Church: revelation is real and comes from God, but it is also slow and human.

Revelation as a Process

Our mortal experience means that a veil separates us from the presence of God. Although we can receive revelation, we sometimes struggle to understand it, interpret its meaning, and put it into practice. The founding meeting of the Church of Jesus Christ of Latter-day Saints took place ten years after the First Vision. When it takes a long time for an initial revelation to bear actual fruit, some of us start to doubt our interpretation of the revelation. While it's good to be prayerfully open to the possibility that we have misunderstood something, it's also important to remember that revelation is a process and takes time. My study of Church history has taught me that our leaders have pursued their planning and decision making "by study and also by faith." Revelation, study, and faith all interweave in the process. For many of us, it seemed as though President Nelson made a lot of rapid changes when he became prophet, but in fact many of those changes had been under consideration for a long time. Church leaders had studied what those changes would look like and, in cases such as two-hour church and the new youth achievement program, they performed pilot programs to test them. In short, they had been counseling together and praying about many of these changes for years.

The 1978 restoration and extension of temple and priesthood blessings for Black Church members is an example of an important revelation taking a great deal of time, thought, and internal struggle. Many faithful Black Saints had suffered deeply from being excluded from priesthood and temple blessings and had pleaded and prayed for a change. Because Church leaders believed such change had to come by revelation and consensus, they sought divine direction. This process proved to be a slow and winding journey, with many obstacles in the path. It crystallized when President Spencer W. Kimball was the prophet. He engaged in an intense fifteen-year phase of prayer, but the process began even earlier, in his youngest years.[3] Some of the obstacles that he had to overcome in seeking revelation existed inside himself. As President Kimball put it, "I had a great deal to fight ... myself, largely," because of his upbringing in Arizona

---

3. On President Kimball's process of questioning, see Edward L. Kimball, "Spencer W. Kimball and the Revelation on Priesthood," *BYU Studies Quarterly* 47, 2 (2008): 35–59.

where he was acquainted with few Black people.[4] Because their experience was distant from his, it took President Kimball many years of training as an Apostle, witnessing the Church's growth in Brazil and Africa, and speaking with Black members before he was, of his own admission, ready to bring the question again before the Lord. He consulted the work of scholars and asked experts for their views in order to educate himself.[5] Other Church leaders and the global Church membership also needed to be educated.[6]

President Kimball's son Edward Kimball wrote that although his father "responded to questions about policy and doctrine with traditional, orthodox explanations, even within his family," it was "clear that inwardly he struggled with the priesthood issues and wished the Lord would permit a change. He felt compassion toward those excluded and perhaps guilt that faithful men were banned from a responsibility and blessing he himself prized."[7] Gordon B. Hinckley, a member of the Quorum of the Twelve Apostles from 1961, said about President Kimball: "Here was a little man, filled with love, able to reach out to people.... He was not the first to worry about the priesthood question, but he had the compassion to pursue it and a boldness that allowed him to act."[8]

This long wrestle took a heavy toll on President Kimball. In the spring of 1978, his wife Camilla Kimball noticed that he seemed distressed and withdrawn. His mood greatly worried her. Even friends and neighbors noticed that President Kimball seemed to be carrying a heavy burden.[9] During

---

4. Kimball, 48. See p. 37 for President Kimball's upbringing in Arizona.
5. Kimball, 46, and 54, footnote 148.
6. Kimball, 43.
7. Kimball, 40.
8. Kimball, quoted on 44, see footnote 110.
9. Kimball, 48–49, 53.

those months, he spent many hours at the temple, early in the morning and late into the night, in discussion with his brethren and in prayer before the Lord. Obtaining this answer to his prayer required humility and the greatest effort of the prophet's mind, body, and spirit. As time passed and he remained persistent, however, he gradually found that the obstacles were diminishing, and "all those complications and concerns [were] dwindling in significance."[10] On June 1, 1978, President Kimball met with the Quorum of the Twelve Apostles in the temple. He told them of his long struggle and of his growing certainty that the Church should extend temple and priesthood blessings to Black Latter-day Saints. He asked them to share their thoughts, and then they prayed together. President Gordon B. Hinckley later described the light they jointly received: "By the power of the Holy Ghost there came to that prophet an assurance that the thing for which he prayed was right, that the time had come ... the voice of the Spirit whispered with certainty into our minds and our very souls."[11] The men embraced in a flood of unity and elation and then hurried to make plans to share the revelation with the world. All worthy members of every race and nation would be eligible to enter the temple, and all worthy men would be eligible to hold the priesthood. Black Latter-day Saints would finally be fully embraced in the blessings of the gospel. When the answer came, the members of the First Presidency and Quorum of the Twelve were united in their rejoicing.

I'll now share two more examples from Church history showing how revelation is a process that is essential to the

10. Quoted in Kimball, 49.
11. Quoted in Kimball, 57.

continuing restoration of the Church. That process can be arduous, even burdensome for a time, before the answers dawn. This is true for revelations that shape the Church and for the personal revelations that shape our lives.

Living in Farmington, Utah, in the late 1870s, 43-year-old Aurelia Spencer Rogers noticed a problem—the boys were rowdy, inconsiderate, and apparently not grounded in the gospel that their elders had sacrificed security, comfort, and relationships to preserve. As Aurelia Rogers looked for solutions to this problem, God whispered to her his approval and encouragement, so she continued to develop the idea of forming a Church organization for children, which has enriched Latter-day Saint lives around the world ever since.

First, Aurelia Rogers shared her ideas with Eliza R. Snow, the General President of the Relief Society, who liked them and described them to Acting Church President John Taylor. The Apostles approved the plan, and Eliza wrote a letter to Aurelia's bishop explaining the matter. Soon, Aurelia had a mandate to gather the children in Farmington and to figure out how an organization for them should function.[12] Looking back, she described how she felt after accepting the calling:

> While thinking over what was to be done for the best good of the children, I seemed to be carried away in the Spirit, or at least I experienced a feeling of untold happiness which lasted three days and

---

12. Aurelia Spencer Rogers, *Life Sketches of Orson Spencer and Others: And History of Primary Work* (Salt Lake City: George Q. Cannon & Sons Co., 1898), 207–8. Excerpted in *The First Fifty Years of Relief Society: Key Documents in Latter-day Saint Women's History*, ed. Jill Mulvay Derr, Carol Cornwall Madsen, Kate Holbrook, and Matthew Grow (Salt Lake City: Church Historians Press, 2016), 341–342.

nights. During that time nothing could worry or irritate me; if my little ones were fretful, or the work went wrong, I had patience, could control in kindness, and manage my household affairs easily.[13]

But those joyous feelings were not permanent. While planning and working for the children, she began to feel unworthy and depressed, so much that she had trouble fulfilling her responsibilities. "I went to my meetings weeping by the way, being humbled to the very earth; so much so, that whatever anyone said afterward in my praise, did not make me feel exalted, or lifted up in my own mind."[14]

Nonetheless, she went on to found what we now call the Primary organization. Maybe *you* wonder, as I have, why she experienced this dark sadness while doing important work. Shouldn't acting on revelation and being on the Lord's errand feel endlessly blissful? Shouldn't it keep negative feelings at bay? This would only be true if Eve and Adam had not eaten that special fruit. In real life, acting on revelation does not promise that we will feel inspired all the time. We did not come to earth for it to be easy to discern answers. The fact that we live in physical bodies and must seek God through the limitations and joys of those bodies is part of why obtaining revelation can be hard. Being embodied is not easy, and working with other people is not easy, but these are two of the major reasons we are here: to have the experience of inhabiting a mortal body and to work with and serve other people.

When my middle daughter was learning to drive, she drove a simulator machine before sitting behind the wheel

---

13. Rogers, *Life Sketches*, 212.
14. Rogers, *Life Sketches*, 214.

of a real car. The real car is much harder to drive; the stakes are so much higher. On the simulator machine if you run a stop sign, it will tell you that you made a mistake and make you start a new round. In real life, if you run a stop sign you could severely injure another person. Driving a real car is dangerous, but it's also the only way to really learn to drive. Living in a body also is dangerous. People, disease, gravity, and our own clumsiness hurt us—they can kill us or wound us in ways that feel even harder than death. But there are lessons that only our bodies can teach us.

Our bodies can also be sources of great joy. For me, physical exercise, making my muscles stronger and my balance more sure, brings joy. Physical joy also comes through the experience of cooking, which is a great source of pleasure to me, a satisfying creative art, and a way to serve others. My body also helps me to express and receive affection—hugs and kisses from loved ones, but even hugs from people who aren't in my closest circle can be wonderful. Maybe you, like me, felt more aware of embodiment's joys when the COVID-19 virus temporarily took some of them away. We learn from the *sorrows* of embodiment as well as from the joys.

For Aurelia Rogers, acting on revelation did not yield uninterrupted happiness. The experience of another Church leader shows that acting on revelation does not guarantee that all the support we need will fall into place either. Ardeth Kapp was the Young Women General President during the 1980s and had experience with this. Sister Kapp was well prepared when she was called as president. She had already worked as a teacher and consultant, been part of the Church Youth Correlation Committee, and served in a Young Women general presidency. Immediately after accepting the calling of Young Women General President, she began to receive revelation. She wrote in her journal, "It seems to me the heavens are opening and thoughts, directions, spiritual promptings are coming clear and fast."[15] Even at that early time, she felt the organization needed a charter statement and a goal system that was based on values. But it took three years of focused effort before the Young Women theme and values were fully created and announced, and five years until the values-based Personal Progress manual came out. Collaboration, execution, and further revelation took time. So did getting approvals.

President Kapp was very good at counseling with others; she called capable people to her board, and they worked collaboratively together. Elder Bednar has taught that different members of a council can have different pieces of revelation, and you need each person's input in order for the whole vision to come together. "The contributions of all of the council members add elements to the inspiration," he said.[16] Former members of President Kapp's board have told me that she was gifted at drawing out the people on her councils. But effective collaboration takes time. The program changes President Kapp oversaw were complex, and getting the details right was slow. There were delays, repetitive extra labor, and other frustrations. For the new Personal Progress program, she called a committee of men and women, most of them married couples, and *they* worked together for two years. Furthermore, President Kapp was president during a time when female officers of the Church did not interact

---

15. Ardeth G. Kapp and Carolyn J. Rasmus, interview by Gordon Irving, 1992, 41, Church History Library. Also p. 59.

16. Panel Discussion (worldwide leadership training meeting, November 2010), https://www.churchofjesuschrist.org/broadcasts/article/worldwide-leadership-training/2010/11/panel-discussion?lang=eng.

much with the First Presidency, as they previously had, and they did not serve on high church committees such as the Priesthood and Family Executive Committee, as they do now. The resulting communication gaps also required extra time and work. "The system was constantly changing," she explained. "You just thought you knew how to do it and now you could do it clean and efficient and save time and maintain quality, and then a new form would come out and there would be a whole new dimension or level of process. Right in the middle sometimes the process would change, and you'd have to start back on item one of twenty-three approvals. So you might have gotten to approval twenty and have to start all over again."[17]

But the result of her perseverance was programs that effectively nurtured the young women of the Church for more than thirty years. Not only were the programs good, but all the people with whom she had counseled understood them well and could help to explain, implement, and in other ways support the new changes. President Kapp's example motivates me because even when she was discouraged, she continued to counsel with others, exercise faith, fast, pray, and work hard. When I read about her experiences, I feel the Spirit testify that she acted on revelation and that God magnified her considerable innate talents through collaboration with other people. If we don't continue to pursue the Lord's guidance, particularly when we encounter difficulties or frustrations, then we might overlook inspired solutions and fail to fix problems. We and others may not learn what the Lord invites us to learn.

---

17. Kapp and Rasmus, interview, 212.

Our Revelations—Receiving and Recording

Learning about other people's revelations can give us insights into our own, especially how our own revelations can make us better at helping others. I have a quotation near my desk to remind me that good thinking and good work take time and careful study. The words are from Simone Weil, a French philosopher who thought a great deal about right and wrong and who made great personal sacrifices to live in ways she determined were morally right. Weil taught, "All wrong translations, all absurdities in geometry problems, all clumsiness of style and all faulty connection of ideas ... all such things are due to the fact that thought has seized upon some idea too hastily and being thus prematurely blocked, is not open to truth."[18]

To make ourselves feel less insecure, we humans like to define things. We often grab onto a definition quickly, because having the definition makes us feel comfortable and safe. As Weil suggests, the problem with rushing things is that we can reach a wrong conclusion. I believe this desire to hastily find and hold tight to a potentially false definition is what leads to some of our greatest sins against one another. These include bigotry, which rears its ugly head in every nation and every political party as we misunderstand each other's intentions and lash out in response. Excessive speed can also lead us to teach a false principle in a lesson or argue on social media in a way that treats someone unfairly.

On the other hand, not everything needs to take a long time. Perfectionism can keep us from ever getting anything

---

18. Simone Weil, *Waiting on God*, Routledge Revivals (Routledge, 2009), 35.

done. Bearing a simple testimony, studying the scriptures with another person, reaching out in ministry—these can be part of our process instead of a perfect end. Our efforts can be imperfect. Prayers can be imperfect. We can be imperfect. In this life we try to improve, but we can't help but make mistakes. That's true of hearing God as well: we will not be perfect in receiving revelation, because it is a process. When perfectionism threatens to halt progress, my husband quotes these wise words attributed to Voltaire: "the perfect is the enemy of the good." What he means to say is that perfectionism can paralyze us and prevent us from accomplishing the good that can result from simply trying.

I'd like to acknowledge how painful it can be when you don't feel adept at receiving and understanding revelation. There are valiant souls among us who obey and seek, who strive to do everything right, yet struggle to perceive revelation from God. That situation can be upsetting. They may feel unworthy, although they are not. They may feel isolated from God and from other members of the Church. I have mourned that even Mother Teresa, a devout and tremendous example of service and spiritual wisdom, felt for long periods that God was distant. In one case, she asked someone she trusted to pray for her that she would do God's will when she herself couldn't hear God's will: "the silence and the emptiness is so great, that I look and do not see,—Listen and do not hear ... I want you to pray for me—that I let Him have [a] free hand."[19]

What do we do if we don't feel we receive answers to our prayers? Some people I deeply admire fall into this category, and I have learned from observing them.

---

19. David Van Biema, "Mother Teresa's Crisis of Faith," *Time*, Aug. 23, 2007, https://time.com/4126238/mother-teresas-crisis-of-faith/.

First, they recognize that some of us have an easier time receiving and understanding revelation than others. For those who struggle to perceive revelation, it may feel as though they are lacking a sense that others have, like the ability to hear a high-pitched sound: some people can hear it, and some people can't. Or they may have minds that constantly supply multiple explanations for their impressions, or many possible answers to spiritual questions. Some people can become overwhelmed with anxious or numb feelings at moments of spiritual intensity, masking the spiritual impressions they hope to receive. In other contexts, each of these traits—the ability to pay close attention, to think creatively, or to avoid getting swept up in excessive emotionalism—can function as a blessing. Often, those who don't easily receive personal revelation possess other gifts, and they use the gifts they do have to serve others.

Next, those who hear the voice of the Lord infrequently can continue to acknowledge all the goodness that comes from church participation. They see the beautiful lives and relationships it fosters. They trust in its goodness. Their trust brings new meaning to Nephi's exhortation to "press forward with a perfect brightness of hope" (2 Nephi 31:20). Elder David A. Bednar described this process as "disciplined endurance ... the result of spiritual understanding and vision, persistence, patience and God's grace."[20] They continue in the everyday practice of their faith, at home and in their church community, even when they do not have strong spiritual manifestations. The familiar discipline of church service, prayer, fasting, and scripture study refines a person's

---

20. David A. Bednar, "Therefore They Hushed Their Fears," *Ensign,* Apr. 2015, 48, https://www.churchofjesuschrist.org/study/general-conference/2015/04/therefore-they-hushed-their-fears?lang=eng.

character, whether or not it is accompanied by spiritual fireworks.

Finally, they are humble. They remember the moments when they have felt the influence of divine power, however slight. Instead of stomping their feet that they don't have more, they appreciate what they do have.

I also want to add a note of hope here. When they served in their respective Relief Society general presidencies, both Sheri Dew and Julie Beck taught that revelation is a skill we can develop. I believe that is true. I have watched a friend who doesn't believe that he has the gift of personal revelation but generously serves anyway. I see thoughts come to him with increasing frequency to act in a particular way. He has learned to trust those thoughts, even if he can't be sure that they are personal revelation. He acts in faith and comes closer to God as a result. His life and those of many others have been enriched by his willingness to try.

Another friend wrote to me,

> I do not experience revelations as feelings of comfort or certainty, and only rarely as insights or answers that come to my mind. However, I have had vivid experiences upon meeting particular individuals, in which a strong impression is conveyed to my heart that I am responsible for offering them love, care, and fellowship. Those moments are powerful and the impressions persistent, and I have come to recognize them as revelations.[21]

These paths I've just described are not my own. One of the great treasures of my life is the spiritual gift of personal

21. Email to Kate Holbrook, April 17, 2020.

revelation. Even so, this gift waxes and wanes. Some weeks I receive insights to remember and act on during several of my prayers. Some weeks I do not. Sometimes I receive less light because I ask vague questions, or I fail to listen. Other times I don't ask or listen well, and I receive direction anyway. And then there are periods when God needs me to work things out on my own, so I ask my friends. In all these stages, I know that where I fall short, I can repent, and God will forgive and also compensate others for my blunders. I trust that God is the architect of the final picture. As my friend Daryl Hoole says, "These are only battles. God has already *won* the war."

By virtue of our membership in this Church, we are called to instruct, inspire, and heal. How could God not want to communicate with us when he needs us to do this work? Not all of us have the skills to easily understand revelation, but I believe even those of us who struggle with personal revelation can grow closer to God in the process of doing good work.

Revelation and the Gathering of Israel

There's a strong relationship between revelation and the gathering of Israel. President Nelson has been encouraging the youth, and all Church members, to participate in this gathering.[22] To my mind, the gathering of Israel means that the whole world will be blessed, not only Church members and

---

22. Russell M. Nelson, "Sisters' Participation in the Gathering of Israel," *Ensign*, Oct. 2018: "I'm extending a prophetic plea to you, the women of the Church, to shape the future by helping to gather scattered Israel"; in Charlotte Larcabal, "A Call to Enlist and Gather Israel," *New Era,* Mar. 2019, n.p., the prophet said, "My dear extraordinary youth, you were sent to earth at this precise time, the most crucial time in the history of the world, to help gather Israel"; Russell M. Nelson, "The Gathering of Scattered Israel," *Ensign,* Oct. 2006: "We gather pedigree charts, create family group sheets, and do temple work vicariously to gather individuals unto the Lord and into their families."

potential Church members. Early members of Relief Society believed the founding of Relief Society came from godly revelation. They were present when Joseph Smith turned the key in the name of God and promised that "this Society shall rejoice and knowledge and intelligence shall flow down from this time— this is the beginning of better days."[23] These early sisters interpreted Joseph's promise to mean that conditions would improve for women throughout the world, not only for themselves. They believed that when Joseph Smith turned that key, he made possible things like the Seneca Falls convention, which was the first women's rights convention in the United States.[24] When I first learned of their belief, I thought it was quaint and sweet but simplistic. As I've grown in understanding, however, I've come to agree with them. I do believe that Joseph Smith's promise of better days has been fulfilled in the advancement of women's wellbeing, and I rejoice in that. And I believe that the fulfillment of his promise is ongoing. For instance, Black and Native American women lagged far behind White women in enjoying the expansion of women's rights in the nineteenth and twentieth centuries, and many still don't fully enjoy those rights today. We can participate in the fulfillment of Joseph's prophecy by widening our circle of concern for *all* women. I believe that the better we become as Saints, the more we can bless people outside of our Church as well as those within. Likewise, we in turn can be open to the good things people outside of the Church have to teach us.

Of course, improvement does not happen overnight.

---

23. Nauvoo Relief Society Minute Book, 40, The Joseph Smith Papers, https://www.josephsmithpapers.org/paper-summary/nauvoo-relief-society-minute-book/63.

24. Sarah M. Kimball, "Reply to 'A Man's Advice about Woman Suffrage,'" *Woman's Exponent*, Dec. 1, 1891, 81.

After the godly revelation that the first Relief Society members experienced regarding their organization, there came the slow and human aspects of learning to understand and act on that revelation. Relief Society in Nauvoo did not last beyond Joseph Smith's death. Sisters brought it back in a few local instantiations in the middle 1850s, but most of these lasted less than four years. Relief Society was not revived Church-wide until after Eliza R. Snow took the assignment to do so in late 1867.[25] These two true things about revelation are evident in the gathering of Israel as seen through the prism of Relief Society: revelation is real, and it is powerful, but it usually takes more time and human effort than we expect or want.

Passages written by the Book of Mormon prophet Nephi have helped me to imagine what the gathering of Israel looks like in terms of a loving God's responsiveness to human needs for safety and comfort: "he gathereth his children from the four quarters of the earth; and he numbereth his sheep, and they know him; and there shall be one fold and one shepherd; and he shall feed his sheep, and in him they shall find pasture" (1 Nephi 22:24–25). I love the image here of all of us, from every part of the earth, finding pasture together, under one perfect, all-loving shepherd. There is a pasture I love that I visit every summer. Horses and cows graze there. The sky, mountains, meadow, trees, and streams are beautiful. the air is clear. The animals have all that they need, and they are safe there. To have all of us in a safe and beautiful place where we are known, seen, and cared for—I want to be in that place, and I want to help others find it.

25. Jill Mulvay Derr, Carol Cornwall Madsen, Kate Holbrook, Matthew J. Grow, eds., *The First Fifty Years of Relief Society: Key Documents in Latter-day Saint Women's History* (Salt Lake City: Church Historian's Press, 2016), 177, 236–240, 266–269.

The godly and the human aspects of revelation are both crucial to the gathering of Israel. Seeking God's will—as it comes through our leaders and to us individually—is how we can find pasture and help others to do so as well. One of the most meaningful experiences of my life has been building bridges with people from countries outside the one I was born to, especially but not exclusively when I was a missionary. Watching God's love through the Holy Ghost transcend linguistic and cultural barriers fills me with hope. That miracle makes me think that every good thing is possible. It strengthens my faith in Nephi's prophecy that through repentance, "all nations, kindreds, tongues, and people shall dwell safely in the Holy One of Israel" (1 Ne 22:28). I long to see all of us dwell safely in the Holy One of Israel, and that promise motivates me to pursue revelation so I can contribute to this process and help more of us find pasture in Jesus.

Histories about Revelation

In some ways, the way we tell history has misled us about how revelation works. There was a long period in American history where we came to think of "useful" history as those stories that gave us people to venerate. We learned to tell histories that only included those considered to be inspirational. This affected the way we told Church history as well—we made it tidier, the people simpler and easier to understand than they really were. We focused almost exclusively, and sometimes to the point of inaccuracy, on the godly version of revelation. But records themselves can be human and they can be untidy. We at the Church History Department are trying to tell stories of real people in all their complexity and acknowledge the moments when things did not go perfectly. In doing so, we are recovering a more whole understanding of past events. Some people welcome this shift. For others, it creates painful challenges. Despite the pain of this transition, I believe it is the right thing to do. Only a few hours after the Church was organized, God commanded the Saints to keep a record. God didn't tell Church leaders only to record the easy times and members' actions that were one hundred percent correct. Since humans are involved in history, that would make for a very short record.

Regardless of the mess and the missteps, I find the love of God in Church history over and over. I see people who are loving and resourceful as they request revelation and work to decipher it. No one is entirely either/or, holy or unholy, good or bad. We are all a mix of our good and bad choices; understanding this can help us to navigate the ongoing process of revelation. We can approach the reception of revelation with more confidence, knowing that everyone feels a bit lost in the wilderness and that the wilderness experience is part of the process God intended for humans. And we can seek light with more humility, knowing that we just don't have all the answers, and in this lifetime we never fully "arrive" at a perfect understanding.

Church history puts real stories in my heart. One of these is the story of my great-great-great-grandmother, whose husband left her repeatedly, and then finally for good, but who nevertheless raised children, crossed the plains, and served as chair of the female council of health in early Utah, where she shared a recipe for medicine that had come to her through a vision. Church history also includes the story of her descendant, my dad, who made good choices and bad choices. Instead of giving in entirely when his bad choices piled up, part of him kept trying to make good choices. He made awkward phone calls to me once or twice a year. His priesthood and temple privileges were restored around the time of his death. The flame of my own courage is strengthened when I think of the courage it took for him to pursue those reinstatements and to place those phone calls to the daughter he had abandoned when she was six weeks old. Coming to terms with his legacy and efforts at love has been a human and godly revelatory experience for me. Even with all the mistakes my dad made, I honor him for the hard things that he did right. His is not a tidy story, but in addition to forewarning me, it also inspires me.

It requires patience and hope to adopt a view of revelation as a counterbalanced process that links our imperfect human efforts with God's loving gift. *By definition*, hope is something we have despite negative past experience, despite evidence that despair may be more rational. Hope is something we choose. When you feel acutely one of the world's problems, you can spend all your energy in anger and criticism, or you can study, pray, and choose to hope in the solutions that come through revelation. Criticism is vital to good thinking, but I believe we must balance it with hope and with positive action. We can hold that hope out in front of us to light our way and to light the way of others.

James Christensen's painting *The Responsible Woman* has been meaningful to me for a long time. Before I left the Missionary Training Center for the Russia Samara Mission, my friend Laura cut it out of a catalogue, mounted it on foam core, and mailed it to me. I took it with me to every apartment. A year or two after I returned, my friend Emilee found a larger version and asked her artist husband to frame it for me for Christmas. I have displayed it in my home ever since.

In the painting, a woman flies through a purple sky at dusk. It doesn't look like she should be airborne: she has multiple things strapped to her body, so that she doesn't drop

"The Responsible Woman" by James Christensen
Image courtesy of Havenlight.

them. One of them is a baby. One of them is a rope. Another is a musical instrument. To light her way in the darkness, she holds a candle aloft. I believe that the candle symbolizes personal revelation, and it is the reason she can fly. It's true that the candle is another thing that she must carry on her overloaded body; it fills her hand and weighs her down. Its flame looks fragile, as if it could sputter out in the breeze. And yet the candle also seems to be lifting and leading her into the darker night above. The two things that are true of the candle are true of revelation: discerning revelation can be slow, heavy work *and* revelation lights and lifts us through the darkness.

⁌

And perhaps there's another lesson in the painting, as well. If I imagine myself as this woman, what is strapped to my body and weighing me down are three daughters and a husband—but they also lift me, so maybe we're all attached to each other by ropes. I carry along a pen and paper. Books. A chef's knife. A salad to deliver. A garden shovel. Someone else's baby, because I like to help younger moms. A list of people to pray for. A vacuum cleaner. A folder of writing to edit. Esther Ackerberg's recipe for Swedish pancakes. Most of the items are things that I love, but all together I can experience them as overwhelming. Revelation helps me to decide which ones can just float along in their ropes, which need immediate care and what kind, which to turn to for renewed hope and energy. The fact that the woman in the painting does not just stand there reminds me that revelation is a process important to navigating this life, and also a journey in its own right. I believe God is waiting to help us and to make us stronger, but he needs us to follow through on answers to the questions he is waiting for us to ask.

Candle flame is contagious. I find that the revelation lighting my life burns brighter the nearer it is placed to the people and histories that I love. My flame of revelation grows in contact with the gospel of Jesus Christ as restored by Joseph Smith and woven into our Church institution by every prophet since, in contact with Latter-day Saint women's experiences from the past two hundred years, in contact with the choices both good and bad that shaped the lives of my ancestors, and in contact with the love of my friends.

HOUSEWORK IS A CRUCIBLE OF DISCIPLESHIP

Which New Testament ghost casts more gloom into the hearts of believing women than any other? More feelings of discouragement, failure, and the impossibility of doing right? Martha, whose sister is Mary, whose brother is Lazarus, is that ghost. But it's not Martha herself who is responsible; it's the shadow of her we have created through our careless conversations about her. We remember Martha for one thing: she complained to Jesus that Mary wasn't helping her make dinner. We don't remember her generosity in spontaneously inviting Jesus and His disciples into her home, nor her display of faith after her brother died. Jesus's response to Martha's complaint gave Christians thereafter, including us, a basis for seeing housework as inferior to study—the life of the mind re-emphasized as superior to that of the body. By extension, those who spent a good part of their lives in housework learned to see their contributions as less-than—and believed that if they complained about unjust divisions of labor, that would be further evidence of their inferiority.

I don't think this interpretive legacy is what Jesus

wanted, because it is inconsistent with His other teachings and behavior. Jesus Himself did housework. The times of Jesus's life that we know the most about are His thirties, the last few years of His life. He doesn't seem to have had a home during those years, but even so He taught us some things about service and housework. He took on the responsibility for thinking ahead about meals—advising His disciples on where to go and what to do about food (at the final Passover, for example). He Himself also cooked, preparing fish on the beach for His disciples. Sometimes, He performed miracles to make sure that people were made comfortable and fed. In the first miracle we know about, He served people at a wedding—turning water into wine at Cana. Two and a half years later, He transformed a few pieces of coarse bread and dried fish into enough to feed thousands. At the Last Supper, He not only prayed over the bread, but broke it Himself and served it to people. He washed His disciples' feet—a symbolic act that was also housework. Washing the feet of guests was one of the least regarded acts of housework Jesus could have chosen to undertake. If a household had servants or slaves, they would be the ones to do any foot washing. Jesus's act of service shows that no housework, no act of care, is beneath God. He showed us that the planning and work of housework are well worth our energy because He performed them even when He didn't have a house. Because housework is an essential means of serving others, I believe He will help us to do it.

With Jesus's actions in mind, I hereby propose a theology of housework. Theology is the study of religious faith and practice, and housework can be a religious practice, something that can bring us closer to God and other people. Like many things that bring us closer to God, housework is a crucible—a container that holds great heat to refine metal. Housework can cause exploitation and, in response, resentment. It is a place that can consume us, either because we spend too much time on it or because we ignore it and the consequences of that neglect eat away at us. Yet housework is also an opportunity to feel grateful for temporal blessings and to do the work of Jesus, which is to serve others. Both things are true about the crucible of housework: it can make us feel inadequate, and it can be an opportunity to understand God more fully, increasing our sense of gratitude and receiving answers to pleas for help.

Demons

Housework can be a teacher, often of hard truths. While cleaning our ward meetinghouse, I have learned more about the perfectionism that impedes my flourishing in other areas of my life. Although I love the communitarian resonance of members sharing church cleaning responsibilities, in practice cleaning the building is hard for me because of the uneven quality of the result. Sometimes the building is left sparkling, and sometimes smudges remain. A man in our previous ward took it upon himself to do all the cleaning and he turned that into a holy practice. I was grateful for his selflessness not only because it meant that Sam and I were freed from helping when our children were little and physical labor already consumed us, but also because he kept the building really clean.

Now when we take our turn cleaning the building, I feel like I never do enough because the building is so large and I'm only there for a couple of hours; I feel like a shirker. Instead of dwelling on the results of my labor, my thoughts focus on what I am not doing. Yes, I am vacuuming the floor of the Relief Society room, but I'm not dusting the moldings and picture frames. Or maybe I am dusting them, but I vacuumed around most of the chairs instead of moving them all out of the way. Or maybe I spent so much time on the Relief Society room that the Primary room received short shrift.

If the main reason I don't like cleaning the church is because I can't do so to perfection, that teaches me about other areas in my life. I don't like wiping down our gas stovetop for a similar reason—I can't do it perfectly. The stovetop usually has some burnt-on something that I can't seem to remove. This is also why I often dislike writing (by "dislike" I mean that I experience it as Purgatory). I choose to let the flaws be more important than any little good my writing might do. This new self-understanding toward which I'm moving feels momentous. My perfectionism likely also discourages the people with whom I live from having a positive experience of housework. I wonder what will happen spiritually as I learn to ease my expectations.

Housework—either the cleaning we do at the church or the cleaning we do in our homes—can expose our buried feelings of inadequacy. This happens for multiple reasons. Maybe we don't do it well enough, or we feel frustrated because some people overcontribute in creating the housework and undercontribute in performing it. (Children are famous for this.) Perhaps more than any aspect of our lives other than eating, housework is repeated every single day. Repeated activity has the most to teach us because we have to face it time after time. Through the daily nature of housework, we confront our personal thinking errors.

We also may confront our guilt—guilt about not doing enough housework, or not doing it perfectly. If we choose to have other people do some of it for us, we must confront the moral questions that surround that choice as well. Here I feel the need to admit that nowadays we usually have someone clean our house once a week. During the height of the COVID-19 pandemic, our work burdens increased instead of decreased, which I think was true for many people. I'd been saying for a long time that there are many benefits of doing all our own housework, like being in tune with what's going on in the house and having the rewarding feeling of accomplishing something ourselves. Sitting in a living room that someone else has dusted and vacuumed is not the same as sitting in a living room that I have dusted and vacuumed. When I have done it, the work means more; it brings me some peace. But after all that, I have to say that if given the choice, I would choose to have cleaners come back. Because the nature of the work is that it is relentless. Doing it myself means giving up something else—some cooking, some writing, going on a walk with Sam or one of my girls, even fulfilling my ministering assignment. I would rather give up the cleaning than those things. But what does that mean for the people I now pay to clean our house? What does it mean for the people who clean the Church History Library, including dusting and vacuuming my office? Does it mean that by choosing to do something else in my home, I devalue the work they do? Part of my response would be to say that I feel grateful to and honor the dignity of those who specialize in cleaning work. I think a large part of finding a moral approach to outsourcing cleaning work is to acknowledge the dignity and expertise of those who perform it. Still, the demon of perfectionism makes me wonder if I am doing enough. If Christ modeled housework as a vital act of caring for others, what does it mean to outsource some of that work to other people?

Other demons vex our thinking about housework. Let's return for a moment to the story of Martha and Mary, and the question of how we spend our time. President Dallin H. Oaks provided a helpful formulation for thinking about our choices with his phrase "good, better, best," which Church members still cite.[1] A narrow interpretation of the Mary and Martha episode would suggest that, by commending Mary, Christ is saying Martha's housework does not matter. This might lead Church members to consider housework as never belonging to President Oaks's "best" category. Seeing housework as a substandard way to spend time leads to real quandaries. Since at least some housework has to be done, considering it a less-worthy place to spend time creates a psychological bind for those performing housework. At least some housework must be done, so we do it, but we interpret the time spent as a loss. Or others decline to help us because *they* view it as a loss. If housework is not a worthy way to spend time, then we do not feel we can bring it to God in prayer, receiving and acting on the personal revelation that might come in response. We feel bad about ourselves for prioritizing something of marginal importance; we don't receive adequate help in our work because others also see it as meaningless; and we don't seek guidance about it from the powers of heaven. Bitterness can flourish in such an atmosphere while spiritual well-being diminishes.

The question of gender roles is another demon in the housework. In my own life it is when I think of domestic labor as lesser that I feel most resentful about it. The gendered nature of housework is one reason that I and others

---

1. Dallin H. Oaks, "Good, Better, Best," *Ensign,* Oct. 2007, https://www.churchofjesuschrist.org/study/general-conference/2007/10/good-better-best?lang=eng.

are particularly vulnerable here. I write books, and I'm married to a man who writes books. When I see him working on his computer while I am doing housework, I think about the extra insights that will go into the world because of the work he's doing and the insights that won't go out into the world because of the work that I am doing. Gendered roles that rigidly assign all housework to women are a primary context for the exploitation and marginalization of women over the centuries. In Virginia Woolf's astute thought experiment, housework is a major reason we don't have the writings of Shakespeare's sister, for instance.[2] Because of housework and childcare, it's easier to get a male scholar to contribute a book to a series or a chapter to an anthology. Women scholars, and women generally, experience their lives as more replete with domestic responsibility (and they often also have more "housekeeping" responsibilities at work). Even today, most men do less housework than women—particularly the emotional and organizational aspects, but also the simple physical labor of it. It's generally women who pick up the bags, coats, and shoes left by the front door or on the kitchen table; manage the after-school activity and snack schedules; teach the children how to clean and what to clean and make sure that they do so; and keep the pantry and refrigerators supplied.[3] Thankfully, my Sam has learned to take responsibility for a substantial portion of the housework. And I have learned that all those tasks I perform matter.

---

2. See Virginia Woolf, *A Room of One's Own* (London: Hogarth Press, 1929).

3. Renata Forste, "BYU Professor Discusses the Legacy of Virginia F. Cutler in Honored Faculty Lecture," March 2, 2017, https://www.youtube.com/watch?v=YXDftQMZQxQ.

Forgiveness

The delicate practice of sharing housework can bring us to Christ through forgiveness. Most of us have at some point in our lives had to share household chores with someone else. Maybe you live in a home with children, and you face housework that is continually undone—wiping kitchen counters or putting away coloring supplies just in time for someone to get them out again and leave tiny paper cuttings all over the table, the chair, the floor. Maybe you live, as my mom does, in a home that was formerly shared and find yourself having to deal with items that you did not bring into the home. Maybe your current relationships still bear the marks of having shared living space and housework with that person. Regardless of how you live now, sharing housework has likely left some kind of mark on you. The principles we can learn from analyzing the connection between sharing housework and gospel living are broad ones: gratitude, perseverance, forgiveness. If you don't share housework with another person right now, I hope you'll be willing to remember a time when you have and will consider the broader implications that come from those concrete situations.

Housework functions most clearly as a spiritual crucible in the regular opportunities it brings us to forgive. Most of us end up with family members who have different conceptions of what "completed housework" means. My friend Emilee says that many things she finds essential just don't make sense to her family. She can't get them to understand the purpose of top sheets, for example. Recently, when her son obediently made his bed, he carefully laid the top sheet over the spread. Housework means negotiating with each other, with time constraints, with the voices in our heads.

Negotiation often skirts the edge of conflict, and it creates frequent moments that call for forgiveness.

Two things are true with forgiveness when it comes to housework: we can't resign ourselves to unremitting victimhood, and we also need to forgive. Both actions are crucial to our well-being: the universal commandment to forgive does not mean accepting exploitive relationships, where the housework is divided so unequally that one person's development or well-being is compromised. In this we have Jesus as our example. When people behaved badly in their relationships, Jesus told them to stop. He didn't hope things would automatically change on their own; he communicated his understanding of right and wrong. Often, he did so subtly. When the disciples were arguing about which one of them was greatest, he responded by undoing the category of "greatest" and, as I understand it, taught them to cut through considerations of status.[4] If we take Jesus as our guide in negotiating housework, we can feel confident in communicating what we understand to be fair and right within our own relationships, especially when others may, like the disciples, need to reconsider inherited assumptions of gender, age, or class status. At the same time, Jesus's example guides us toward a gentle approach in these conversations around housework. We aim to teach and persuade rather than coerce and shame.

While housework is a commonplace part of life, long-term overwork can do serious harm to a person's potential to contribute to the world and to experience joy in life. Martha Hughes Cannon (1857–1932) was an early Latter-day Saint suffragist, state senator, and physician. She wrote to

---

4. Luke 9:46–48.

her friend Barbara Replogle in 1884, "'Tis not the bringing of noble spirits into the world ... that dwarfs talent, and retards her intellectual advancement but it is the multiplicity of household drudgery... and the conformity to the vile customs of modern society. Barbara even if we have to be poor let us ... strive to become women of intellect, and endeavor to do some little good while we live in this protracted gleam called life."[5]

Cannon's position was that housework endangered the pursuit of excellence. She was right. Today, I could fill my life with so much housework that there would be no time left to write or study or play. I can imagine that housekeeping in Utah during the nineteenth century could become all-consuming. In fact, Brigham Young and Mary Isabella Horne, a prominent Relief Society leader and women's suffragist, had begun late in 1869 a retrenchment program that encouraged women to dress simply and to prepare uncomplicated meals. One of their stated goals was to free women's time from needless domestic labor, so more of it could be spent studying the gospel and in other "edifying" civic pursuits. Their message may have been that housework was a necessary evil, not edifying in and of itself. But maybe they only meant to safeguard against too much housework. As Cannon recognized, the "multiplicity of household drudgery" can stunt a person's talents and intellect or dampen her joy in "this protracted gleam called life." Such a situation might call for serious and direct efforts to rebalance housework in a relationship.

Still, the constant repetition of housework means that

---

5. Martha Hughes Cannon to Barbara Replogle, May 1, 1885, Martha Hughes Cannon Collection, 1883–1912, LDS Church Archives, Salt Lake City.

sometimes our attempts to negotiate housework won't be resolved perfectly. We will have to forgive, again and again. If that forgiveness is offered unwillingly, we can find ourselves holding on to a grudge. A revelation on mercy and forgiveness given to Joseph Smith during a contentious period among Church members reads, "I, the Lord, will forgive whom I will forgive, but of you it is required to forgive all men."[6] It may be hard to accept that the Lord wants us to forgive everyone, though there is comfort in knowing that he will judge some of them. But if that is the case, why not allow us to hold a grudge? Are we justified in begrudging housework? To answer that question, we need to think about what comes from holding a grudge: we might experience a feeling of superiority, or a feeling of restoring balance in the universe. The feeling of superiority is not conducive to growing, loving relationships, so we can discard that as a justification for resentment. A feeling of restoring balance in the universe, on the other hand, is good. But the reality is that we don't actually achieve balance through exercising our own judgments against people, because our vision is narrow and flawed. I may feel justified in my angry grudge against my partner over laundry or dishes, but my perspective is painfully limited in comparison to God's understanding of each of us. Really, I think the only way to trust that there is balance in the universe—even when it comes to something as ordinary as housework—is to let God do the judging. If this is the case, then the scripture is true—let God forgive whom he wants and let us forgive everyone. Unlike the work of balancing the cosmic scales of the universe, which lies outside our ability to understand or achieve, striving for humility

---

6. D&C 64:10.

and charity does lie within our compass. Trying to forgive, with humility and love, is a more reliable path to peace—in housework and in life.

Gratitude

One of the things I particularly value about the Latter-day Saint tradition is our understanding that the physical is spiritual. In fact, we regard the physical challenges of our mortal existence as a major reason why we are here. Housework is a daily, unending physical challenge for us: we wash clothes, only to see them get dirty hours (or minutes) later; we cook food, only to have to do it again when hunger pangs strike once more. Since housework is godly work, we can ask for and receive spiritual promptings about how to prioritize and accomplish it. We can ask in prayer for clarity about how much we really need to do and what we can let go. We can remember that two things are true: housework is physically and psychologically burdensome, and housework is a daily opportunity to seek and receive spiritual succor.

In the early twenty-first century, BYU professor Kathleen Slaugh Bahr analyzed verses in the Book of Moses that articulate the spiritual underpinnings of housework.[7] Bahr noted that "God did not curse Adam; He cursed *the ground* to bring forth thorns and thistles." The cursing of the ground forced Adam to labor, but it was not a curse *of* Adam but rather an opportunity *for* him. As Bahr pointed out, the previous verse says: "Cursed shall be the ground *for thy sake*."[8] Grappling

---

7. The Book of Moses is a Latter-day Saint augmentation of Genesis from the Hebrew Bible. Pondering the contents of the Hebrew Bible, Joseph Smith added new material and interpretation of the ancient text through a revelatory process.

8. Moses 4:23–24. Kathleen Slaugh Bahr and Cheryl A. Loveless, "Family Work," *BYU Magazine*, Spring 2000, https://magazine.byu.edu/article/family-work/. See also Nancy Rollins Ahlander and Kathleen Slaugh Bahr,

with housework has been a part of the human experience from the beginning, and it really can be "for our sake." Our approaches to housework can bring us closer to God. We can pray for help to let go of the resentments that housework might bring into our lives, and we can learn to speak openly and still with love about our feelings with those who do not adequately share in this necessary and potentially spiritual work.

Life is a social experience and our beliefs have much to do with relationships. The work of salvation is the work of relationship. My friend Alice Faulkner Burch remembers her mother imparting important life lessons at the same time she taught her how to cook and clean, so performing the tasks became tied in her memory to those insights. For example, Alice remembers her mother teaching her, as they washed dishes together, strategies for responding emotionally to racism. The act of doing dishes now brings back the wisdom her mother shared while they worked together.[9] We can lay the challenges that housework brings into our lives at the altar of prayer—to ask for help and then to listen. We pray to join in the work, to be generous, and also to forgive.

Setting aside the quality of other people's contributions to housework, performing the work ourselves can foster gratitude, which also brings us closer to God. Doing housework makes me grateful for our house, our car, our garden. When I serve people, I treasure them more. There's a related process with things: when I take care of things, I value them more. This can be spiritually dangerous if we take it too far. Jesus warned, "Lay not up for yourselves treasures upon

---

"Beyond Drudgery, Power, and Equity: Toward an Expanded Discourse on the Moral Dimensions of Housework in Families," *Journal of Marriage and Family* 57, no. 1 (February 1995): 54–68.

9. Alice Faulkner Burch, text message, Feb. 16, 2020.

earth, where moth and rust doth corrupt, and where thieves break through and steal ... for where your treasure is, there will your heart be also."[10] But valuing the household things I care for can also be spiritually uplifting when it takes the form of gratitude. When I have taken extra care with wiping off the kitchen counters so that they shine, I feel grateful for the shine, grateful for the counters, and for the whole kitchen that provides a comfortable place with clean running water and good-smelling dish soap and nutritious food stored away in cupboards and the refrigerator. For me, housework is often an expression of gratitude for the abundance of my life. I feel this when it's my turn to clean at church too. Approaching the building through cleaning eyes lets me notice more of its details: the moldings, the artwork, and the light fixtures. I feel more ownership and appreciation for the building because I have spent more time trying to make it a positive environment for my fellow Saints.

It's true that keeping up with everything is hard, sometimes exhausting, and I have my own coping techniques. I start laundry on a Tuesday evening and try to have it clean, folded, and put away before bedtime on Wednesday so that it doesn't always hang over my head. My family members, who create four-fifths of the laundry, do the folding and putting away. My friend and I cook for each other's households. I make extra food on Mondays and she on Thursdays, an arrangement we both love. Having a schedule that I know will keep me from being overwhelmed with cooking and cleaning helps me to remain grateful for my family and our home.

It also helps to have certain housework rituals that can

---

10. Matthew 6:19, 21.

bring gratitude closer to mind. My friend Laura gathers dirty dishes into her sink, then wipes off her counters with wide slow motions, like she's singing a love song. I have lately taken to reading in the kitchen late in the evenings. Because the kitchen needs lots of cleaning every day, when sitting there I inhabit a place that I have just cared for, and it feels deeply comforting to be there. I think of the closet I organized at my grandparents' cabin last summer, and my heart fills with softness.

I don't mean to suggest that all people are built this way, although I know many who are. What I'm trying to say is that for some of us, housework isn't always drudgery. Sometimes housework is drudgery and sometimes it is a gift. In her autobiography *Heaven is Here*, burn victim Stephanie Nielson eloquently described how, in the early stages of her recovery, she yearned to shop for groceries and cook for her family.[11] When I was having eye surgeries, I couldn't keep things clean on my own, and I suffered over this. Often, now, when I pull out the vacuum, I feel grateful that I can.

For me, the garden is the place where I most clearly see housework as the gift it is—though even that gift has its costs. I have trouble sleeping in the spring because of my garden, wondering whether the mulberry seedpods will harm the grass, wondering whether new mulberry trees will try to establish themselves in the vegetable plot. There's so much to think about: how the plants are doing, how the beds look now. Where do we need a bit of white, of black? How can I get more height in the spring display? As the novelist Jamaica Kincaid so aptly described, "How agitated I am

---

11. Stephanie Nielson, *Heaven Is Here: An Incredible Story of Hope, Triumph, and Everyday Joy* (New York: Hachette Books, 2012).

when I'm in the garden, and how happy I am to be so agitated. How vexed I often am when I'm in the garden, and how happy I am to be so vexed. What to do?"[12]

I try not to read gardening books or magazines within ninety minutes of bedtime; they are far too stimulating. But sometimes I can't resist. Even when I do resist, it is hard with my head on the pillow and soft sheets under my chin not to let my thoughts wander to the flower and vegetable beds just outside my windows. I focus well when I am actually in the garden, where there is only digging, pulling, clipping, and observing. Working in the garden brings me soundly into the present moment. I've read other gardeners, the kind that also like to write, reflect about this. For me, gardening also brings a spiritual rootedness. Gardening is what my people do; it is where I am from.

My mother wished she had paid more attention to her own father's garden, which she remembers as extraordinary. I declined my mother's invitations to help in the garden when I was growing up. I remember her working out there long after dark, the sounds of her moving the hose, watering the pots, coming in through the open patio door along with the evening breezes from Rock Canyon to the east of us. Sounds and breezes together added to the comfort of my repose on our blue velvet couch. At last, she would come inside with a look of deep contentment—until she saw I had taken advantage of her distraction to watch *Love Boat* and *Fantasy Island*—both off limits.

Now I am the one outside after dark, trying to get the early weeding and planting done before the summer heat sets

---

12. Jamaica Kincaid, *My Garden (Book)* (New York: Farrar Straus Giroux, 1999), 14.

in. My Latter-day Saint neighbor across the street suggested a headlamp for after-dark gardening, so you can distinguish new plants from young weeds and keep your hands free. Like Adam, I labor by the sweat of my brow. But it is not a curse. It is an opportunity to forgive the ground for its weeds, to seek the succor of heavenly parents, and to revel in the richness of the black earth. Later, I will sweep that dirt from my kitchen floor. And it is all a gift.

FORGIVING AND REMEMBERING

My first Sunday as a missionary in Russia, I rode an old Soviet streetcar with my mission companion to a still-active meeting house for the Communist Party. Although trees were flowering around the Provo Missionary Training Center when I had left a few days earlier, this April 1993 morning in Samara looked bleak. The temperature required my warmest coat with a scarf and gloves. Trees displayed neither flowers nor buds and not even a crocus stood to promise spring.

I loved it.

Entering the meeting room where we were to have church, I first rushed to a bank of windows through which I could see the midsections of several dozen still-leafless trees, hundreds of them with stark white trunks and black branches. "Trees like these inspired Tolstoy," I thought to myself. I decided they were white birches, since that seemed the most romantic arboreal conclusion (and I think they actually were). Then I turned around to see what the other missionaries were doing. They set up a table and draped it with white cloth, pulling the linens, sacrament trays, loaf of bread, and bottles of water from their navy and black Jansport backpacks. A white bust of Vladimir Lenin sat on the podium in the center front of the room, until an elder carefully took it down and stowed it away, taping a picture of Jesus to the podium instead. The room had dark wood paneling and, without Lenin, somewhat resembled church meeting houses I'd attended growing up. Pictures of Jesus didn't hang from the podiums at home, but I understood the impulse to position one here. You couldn't just remove the image of a person like Lenin; you had to replace it with something to restore the atmosphere.

Lenin's image created a negative feeling because he was responsible for a lot of death and suffering. He was the leader of the Bolshevik Revolution in Russia, the founder of the Communist Party, and a strong influencer of the Communist worldview. He constructed a political system in which it was acceptable to kill an enemy who posed a threat. Anyone in the country could be imprisoned and even sentenced to death without a trial. During a period called the Red Terror, anywhere from tens of thousands to over a million eoplee were killed. Because of secrecy and censorship, the numbers are only estimates. But in any case, Lenin not only performed devastating deeds himself, but set up systems in which terrible practices would continue for decades after his death. I didn't have to live with Lenin as a political leader, but I have loved and mourned with the descendants of those who did. His legacy was not one to easily set aside, nor was it prudent to forget. Should a similar despot appear, we would need to remember what we learned from the ravages of this one and be ready to stop the next.

As I have made my way through adulthood, there have been situations and people hard enough to forgive that just removing them from sight was not enough—I needed to replace them with images of Jesus. Whether we've had to deal with the minor vexations of individuals or the major terrors of civil war, looking to Jesus to restore what people have damaged and replace what they symbolize is the most effective response. Jesus offers the most complete healing. I believe finding healing in Jesus is also best for those around me, from my own household to the more distant souls with whom I share this planet.

But what does it mean to find healing in Jesus from wrongs inflicted by others? Both things are true here. We believe forgiveness, which Jesus makes possible, is the only way for us to heal and make progress as individuals and as communities, large and small. At the same time, we can't simply cover up and forget about serious wrongdoing. We don't want to excuse behavior that is manipulative, abusive, or even just unloving, because we don't want to facilitate that behavior. How do we protect ourselves from pernicious people and systems? How do we become whole in their wake? How can we forgive and remember?

Becoming People Who Forgive

Other people are capable of making us feel misery and joy, and the potential for hurt is particularly strong when those other people are our children or other family members. Children require a fair amount of work, and caring for them can wear us out. In a marriage relationship, having children to feed and clothe, instruct and comfort, can feel like too much to do along with everything else life requires. This can create real tension in marital and other relationships, which provides many opportunities to practice forgiving. We also want to be forgiven ourselves.

When my three daughters were little, I confided in my friend Emilee my concern that these little beings I loved so very much would later resent me for my parenting mistakes, even though I was trying so hard to do everything right. I told her that I took photos even though it sometimes took away from the moment, and even though I felt overwhelmed by the thought of later choosing, printing, and compiling the photos. I felt the work was worth doing because it would show them the birthday celebrations, sandwich parties, and other attempts I made to create for them a happy childhood. Emilee's response shone the sun on the shadows of my worries. Her older sister-in-law had said she just tried to teach her children to forgive, then hoped they would forgive her as well as everyone else. That approach struck me as our best chance for future happy relationships and my children's best chance to get along well in life. Teach them to forgive, and then all of the goodness can fall into place. When I thought that way, I felt worry slide from my mind down to my shoulders and then off and away.

In my concern to construct a positive past for my daughters, I was trying to manipulate the future. That doesn't sound like a worthy endeavor and in fact it was not. Usually, as a historian, I work at the other end of the equation, representing and analyzing the actual past of someone else. The work is difficult, a quandary over trying to be honest and fair. We want to show the past accurately without forgetting and perpetuating detrimental behaviors. We also want to allow for forgiveness.

Moroni wrote about this in the Book of Mormon. His father edited the authors' different writings, compiled them together, and then handed them to Moroni. Following the destruction of his people, Moroni was all alone as he took care of the Nephite records, translated the Jaredite record, and added some thoughts of his own while waiting to die.

As someone who writes and edits myself, I can imagine how he felt. His main reason for being alive was to protect that record, and at the same time he was acutely aware of the shortcomings in it. Would this collection that he and his dad had sacrificed for be good enough? He wrote in the title page: "if there are faults they are the mistakes of men; wherefore, condemn not the things of God." He asked readers there to forgive, to overlook any weaknesses in the book, and to not confuse the human shortcomings in the book with God's works. He wrote something similar, only with a promise, in Mormon 8:12: "And whoso receiveth this record, and shall not condemn it because of the imperfections which are in it, the same shall know of greater things than these." What a lesson that is. If we are able to overlook the errors of these writers who devoted themselves to doing God's work, but were human and did so imperfectly, then we will get to know even greater things than are in the Book of Mormon.

Thinking about the forgiveness that Jesus makes possible, we can go all the way back to the scene where it first became necessary, in the Garden of Eden. Adam and Eve's eating the fruit was essential to the purpose of life. The Book of Mormon prophet Lehi described the Fall as he spoke of spiritual truths with his sons at the end of his life. Lehi taught that if Adam and Eve had not eaten the fruit of the tree of life, "they would have remained in a state of innocence, having no joy, for they knew no misery; doing no good, for they knew no sin." That last part of the quotation is really interesting to me: "Doing no good, for they knew no sin" (2 Nephi 2:23). According to these lines, there really can't be growth, or goodness, or joy, or fulfilling the purpose of life—or, apparently, taking cookies to your neighbor—without misery and sin.

A few verses later, verse 26 explains that all this freedom to have joy and misery, to do good and bad, necessitates having a Savior. Otherwise, the sin and the misery would obliterate the good works and the joy. Here is the description of how the Savior saves us from sin and misery: "Because that they are redeemed from the fall they have become free forever, knowing good from evil; to act for themselves and not to be acted upon" (2 Nephi 2:26). Sometimes people have treated us so badly that it feels like they restrict our agency, our ability to act, but this verse promises the atonement can make us free forever. I believe this teaching, and I am not alone.

Forgiveness is one of the ways we can exercise the ability to act. Although the opportunity to forgive comes in everyday circumstances as well as dramatic ones, I'll share a dramatic example because it helps to put others in perspective. This story comes from a collection of global oral histories that are helping to expand our understanding of Latter-day Saint experience beyond the Wasatch Front. "Charity" is a Rwandan Latter-day Saint whose husband was falsely imprisoned for almost ten years for supposedly hiring an assassin to kill a Tutsi woman as part of the 1994 genocide. Charity's husband was set free when the real perpetrators came forward and admitted their crime, but her family was still left with a tremendous amount of pain following the suffering and separation caused by her husband's imprisonment. She chose to make forgiveness a part of her healing. She told the accuser that she forgave him, and she later described forgiveness as a reconciliation. She explained that while bad acts cause separation, forgiveness achieves the opposite. "I forgive you. You forgive me. Then we come like we were brothers and sisters, and we don't have any separation between us. That separation, you just erase it." The act of forgiveness not only benefits the perpetrator but also the person who was wronged. "When you hate someone, you have this burden on you," she said. "But when you forgive, you feel free. You feel free!"[1]

Forgive But Don't Forget

When the scriptures discuss our forgiving one another, they don't talk about forgetting. God occasionally promises to forget our mistakes (Isaiah 43:25, Jeremiah 31:34, Hebrews 10:17), but humans aren't directed to forget. This is a crucial aspect of the two things that are true here: Jesus makes forgiving and healing possible, but we don't want to excuse destructive behaviors or encourage the possibility of repeating them by forgetting.

Forgiveness must co-exist alongside accountability. I see forgiving but not forgetting as the only way through this situation. Familiar expressions in English make us think "forgive and forget" are words that naturally belong together, but they don't appear together in the scriptures. Sometimes I know for certain they should *not* be together. Whether I write about American history or women's history or food history or Church history, which is my main job, I can't just forget about things people have done wrong in the past. My job is to study and figure out the truth of what happened, as close as I can come to it through the sources that I have. The lessons we learn from history only come in a true way when we represent history accurately. Also, if we took out all the human mistakes from history, it would be really boring to read.

But it's difficult to know how to treat people fairly, whether in everyday life or when writing history books.

---

1. "Charity," interview by Amy Hoyt, Aug. 7, 2016, *Women, Religion and Transitional Justice: Ethnographic Research in South Africa and Rwanda,* project conducted through the University of the Pacific.

I wrote at the beginning of this essay about some of the terrible things that Lenin did. But because I aspire to write history that is fair and complete, I also acknowledge how smart he was and how much he cared about the awful unfairness that peasants in Russia experienced. He was kicked out of law school for participating in a student demonstration, but he continued to study on his own and managed to take the law exams. He earned first place on the exams, but instead of finding a job that could earn him respectability or plenty of money, he put his new degree to work representing peasants. Seeing their struggles, and the way legal systems were set up to always disadvantage them, motivated his revolutionary work. He wanted to create a better world for those who suffered the most. Maybe knowing this additional information will give you a fuller understanding of Lenin and help you to learn more from his life, such as how good motives can blind us to the evil methods we use in pursuit of those goals.

The difficulties inherent to forgiveness and fair representation flourish in the field of history—whether we participate in that field as readers, writers, or makers. I think I've made my view clear, which is that discipleship calls us to forgive past actors, but not to forget their bad actions and the harm they've done (and sometimes continue to do), be it on the large stage of world history or the intimate arenas of family history and personal history. In fact, I believe those bad actions of the past, and the villainous systems and thinking patterns some of them created, must be remembered to safeguard the present. If we don't remember Lenin and teach our children the values he failed to practice himself, we could find ourselves with another Lenin. Forgetting makes it possible for new perpetrators to wreak havoc.

But I do find it challenging to do justice to people of the

past. Writing history is spiritual work, and I believe it should be an exercise in empathy. I believe that I should treat those of the past with the same empathy that I promised at my baptism to show the living people around me. Still, especially in oral presentations, I've had to fight the temptation to poke a little fun or depict people from the past as quaint or ignorant. I've had to repent from doing so early in my career. And now that I'm more practiced at resisting that temptation, I have to forgive the other historians that I see mistreating past figures in those ways that I used to do. Or worse than I used to do. Sometimes our own "virtues," even good-faith efforts to improve ourselves, can be the occasion for yet more repentance if we become judgmental of those who haven't walked our path.

One reason we need to forgive people of the past is because they lived in circumstances that are different from ours. They were raised with sometimes similar but other times different values. They experienced particular threats and were taught different ways to respond to those threats. Judging people of the past by the standards of today is seen as a bad thing in the field of history. A past president of the American Historical Association explains that such judgment "encourages a kind of moral complacency and self-congratulation. Interpreting the past in terms of present concerns usually leads us to find ourselves morally superior ... our forebears constantly fail to measure up to our present-day standards."[2] But there are other historians who argue that sometimes we have to say something in the past was inexcusably bad—marital rape, for example—and that makes sense, too.

2. Lynn Hunt, "Against Presentism," *Perspectives on History,*" May 1, 2002, https://www.historians.org/publications-and-directories/perspectives-on-history/may-2002/against-presentism.

Darius Gray is someone who has taught me to navigate the balance between avoiding anachronistic judgments and acknowledging bad behaviors in the past to keep us from perpetuating them. Darius joined the Church at a time when it prohibited people of African descent from receiving their temple endowment and men from being ordained to the priesthood. He found out about these prohibitions the night before his baptism. Darius remembered that night in an interview in 2017:

> My impression was that I had been duped. My mom's concerns that she had voiced earlier were valid. I sat there and I listened and I thought, "There's no way in hell I'm going to be baptized tomorrow." I went home. I couldn't tell Mom because I knew how she felt. . . . So I entered into prayer. After closing that prayer, I just tossed and turned in bed, then entered into prayer a second time.
>
> The truth is I received personal revelation. I did not see angelic beings; I did not see God the Father or the Savior; but I heard—I heard—"This is the restored gospel and you are to join." There was no mention of the priesthood restriction—whether it was of God or of man or whatever—just, "This is the restored gospel."
>
> Based on that and based on my Christian upbringing—and when you hear that voice, that voice of Deity, it's not the burning of the bosom—you have a very clear choice. So the next day, I was baptized.[3]

---

3. Darius Gray, "An Interview About the Genesis of Change in the LDS Church," *Faith Matters* (podcast), 13 Dec. 2017, https://faithmatters.org/the-genesis-of-change-in-the-lds-church-an-interview-with-darius-gray/.

His early years in the Church were "lonely." When asked if he second guessed his decision to be baptized, he responded: "No. Couldn't. Again, that voice—the strength of that has carried me through. Whatever else has happened—and there has been the good, the bad, and the in-between—it's all been based on that one experience on the evening of December 25th, Christmas day, 1964." In 1971, Darius was one of the founding leaders of the Genesis Group for African American Church members so they could support one another, and this group still exists today.

Darius has been a wonderful teacher for Saints of all racial backgrounds, and one of the things he taught was that forgiving doesn't mean forgetting. He said it this way, "The first step toward healing is the realization that the problem exists, even among some of us in the Church, as President Hinckley pointed out. We cannot fix that which we overlook or deny. Our attitudes toward others of a different race or of a different culture should not be considered a minor matter. Viewing them as such only affirms a willingness to stay unchanged."[4] His line "we cannot fix that which we overlook or deny" seems particularly important to the second thing that is true in this essay. While we need to forgive, we should not deny that prejudices existed.

Seeing Each Other as Children of God

Forgiveness also requires that we see one another as children of God. Darius Gray taught that in addition to acknowledging the problem of prejudice, we need to recognize it in ourselves and learn new ways "to approach those who may appear different.... See the child of God for who he or she

---

4. Darius Gray, "Moving Forward Together," *Ensign*, Jun. 2018, https://www.churchofjesuschrist.org/study/ensign/2018/06/commemorating-the-1978-revelation/moving-forward-together?lang=eng.

really is—a brother or sister—rather than someone different." And then he advises that we listen "to truly hear from those we consider as 'the other.'"[5]

The brief book of Enos gives us an example of a good man who at one time said harsh things about a group of people different from him, but who was led to see their spiritual worth as the Spirit of God worked on his soul.[6] In his record, Enos called the Lamanites "wild, and ferocious, and a blood-thirsty people, full of idolatry and filthiness" (Enos 1:20). He didn't like the way they dressed or the raw food they ate or the tents they slept in. He also described the settled, agrarian habits of the Nephites, and he didn't criticize that approach—it was the way he thought best to live. The fact that his own Nephite people and the Lamanites were always trying to kill each other must have contributed to his attitude about the Lamanite people as a whole. For me, Enos's description of what he didn't like about the Lamanites and their lifestyle is hard to read. It is a reminder that even though Enos was inspired, he was still vulnerable to the us-vs-them mentality that tempts all of us humans and has misled us throughout human history.[7]

At the same time, Enos was moved to pray for the Lamanite people who were trying to kill him and to also see the faults in his own people, who were trying to kill the

---

5. Gray, "Moving Forward Together,"

6. See Sharon J. Harris, *Enos, Jarom, Omni: a brief theological introduction* (Provo, Utah: Neal A. Maxwell Institute, 2020), 18–48.

7. At "Be One," the 40th anniversary celebration of the 1978 revelation on the priesthood, President Dallin H. Oaks said, "Racism is probably the most familiar source of prejudice today, and we are all called to repent of that. But throughout history, many groups of God's children are or have been persecuted or disadvantaged by prejudices, such as those based on ethnicity or culture or nationality or education or economic circumstances." His address was printed in "A Cause for Celebration," *New Era*, August 2018, https://www.churchofjesuschrist.org/study/new-era/2018/08/be-one/a-cause-for-celebration?lang=eng.

Lamanites. The spiritual work he did in repenting and trying to understand and perform God's will resulted in his caring about the welfare of both Nephites and Lamanites, as well as their future descendants (1:13). Enos was reminded that the Lamanites and the Nephites were kin, and he prayed "with many long strugglings" that "they might be brought unto salvation" (1:11, 13). Enos also had clarity of thought in identifying behaviors, among both peoples, that separated humans from God—hatred, killing, pride. In one verse, he described his own people as "stiffnecked, [and] hard"—or slow—"to understand" (1:22). There is so much meaning in those words: he liked the cultural customs of his people—the ways they ate and farmed and put down roots—but he couldn't understand why they wouldn't accept God's words as having more wisdom than their own thoughts.

What I'm trying to say here is that repentance and charity are crucial for learning to do right by each other as fellow children of God. Even though Enos's time and place created in him a negative view of the Lamanite people, repentance led him to grow and to pray for them as "my brethren" (1:11). As he came to pray for his enemies, it appears that repentance helped Enos to forgive. I have noticed a similar tendency in myself. Feelings of guilt and defensiveness keep me from forgiving, while letting myself move into repentance makes me eager for it.

Like so many others, I have wrestled with forgiveness and remembering in my own life. A couple of weeks after we moved to a new home, I saw a dark spot at the side of my vision. I realized that my left eye had felt irritated for several months, so I made a morning appointment with my eye doctor. He misdiagnosed the problem, but by the end of the day, having seen two other specialists, I learned that I had cancer in my left eye. Best case scenario, one of the doctors told my husband Sam on the phone that evening, I would lose my eye. Worst case, I would die in a few months.

Our house was still chaotic—things in boxes, bookshelves waiting in the kitchen for installation in the study, dust everywhere, aggravating my asthma. There was also chaos in my self. When and how much should we tell the girls? What would it be like to lose an eye? How should we spend our time together? When would it come to an end?

Losing an eye was rough, it turned out, but also lucky because the cancer hadn't spread at that point. Doctors had warned me that "enucleation" was a big surgery with a long recovery. What I didn't expect was that it would also be really hard on our marriage.

I ended up having three surgeries over several months, and by the time I started to feel better physically, regain my balance, and relearn to drive, I found I was angry with Sam. He was (in his words) a vaguely autistic workaholic who didn't get involved with keeping house. Facing the prospect of death had brought to the surface feelings of resentment that I'd been trying to ignore for years.[8]

We got some counseling. We spent some difficult months learning to communicate better with each other, and I made clear that I would no longer shoulder so much of the housework. Sam did the thing so hard for most humans to accomplish: he made major changes. He agreed to pick up more, to help with the dishes, and to start making dinner, doing the planning and the shopping for that meal, once a week. We also started having weekly dates. We acknowledged the pain and anger in our relationship. We forgave

8. Kate and Sam share this experience in "The Evolving Story of a Marriage," *All In*, an *LDS Living* podcast, episode 136, June 23, 2021, URL https://www.ldsliving.com/all-in/samuel-brown-and-kate-holbrook-the-evolving-story-of-a-marriage. Kate also shared in "Living with Kids," *Design Mom* (blog), 1 September 2022, https://designmom.com/living-with-kids-kate-holbrook/.

each other, but we remembered what had shaken our marriage so that it wouldn't happen again.

In pursuit of this vision where we all come together through Jesus to lift each other up, where we forgive and remember, I want to be clear that we remember so we can improve. When remembering becomes valorizing of past bad actors, it would be better to forget. Writer Clint Smith captured in vivid terms how the remembering can feel when it's a valorization of hate.

> Every time I return home, I drive on streets named for those who would have wanted me in chains. Go straight for two miles on Robert E. Lee. Take a left on Jefferson Davis. Make the first right on Claiborne. Translation—go straight for two miles on the general who slaughtered hundreds of Black soldiers who were trying to surrender. Take a left on the President of the Confederacy who made the torture of Black bodies the cornerstone of his new nation. Make the first right on the man who permitted the heads of rebelling slaves to be put on stakes and spread across the city in order to prevent the others from getting any ideas.
>
> What name is there for this sort of violence? What do you call it when the road you walk on is named for those who imagined you under a noose? What do you call it when the roof over your head is named after people who would have wanted the bricks to crush you?[9]

---

9. "A Poet Reflects on How We Reckon—or Fail to Reckon—with The Legacy of Slavery," *Fresh Air,* Dec. 28, 2020, https://www.npr.org/2020/12/28/949989411/a-poet-reflects-on-how-we-reckon-or-fail-to-reckon-with-the-legacy-of-slavery. Clint Smith is also the author of *How the Word is Passed: A Reckoning with the History of Slavery Across America* (Boston: Little, Brown, 2021).

Memorializing such controversial figures not only damages those whose ancestors suffered at the hands of those very people, but it damages everyone. Because buildings, streets, and monuments celebrate these figures, such honor can also threaten to perpetuate the violence they wrought. At the same time, the topic of remembering past leaders is complex; were we to require that all of them were perfect, there would be no one to remember. I don't know how we decide who is bad enough that their public, physical reminders should be removed. Certainly, those Smith described should be. Somewhere in the midst of forgiving and not forgetting, and listening, lies the answer for others.

I'll close with a final story about Jane Neyman. Jane was raised in western Pennsylvania and was baptized into the Church in 1838. In 1840, she joined the Saints in Nauvoo, where her husband died, and she was left in extreme poverty. A few months after the Relief Society was organized, she asked to become a member (potential members had to ask to join back then). But her daughters had been manipulated by a man named Chauncey Higbee, resulting in a sexual scandal, and Jane was rejected as a member of Relief Society. Many of us would find that rejection hard to forgive, since the scandal was no fault of Jane's. But Jane stayed with the Church, came West with the Saints, and ended up helping to establish the Relief Society in Utah, including serving as a Relief Society president. Twenty-five years after she was rejected in Nauvoo, she gave a talk in Beaver, Utah, about forgiveness, where she noted:

> It seemed to be the unanimous agreement of the Spirit that presided over the meeting that tattling and slander should die a natural death; that charity, which covereth a multitude of sins, which thinketh

no evil, and suffereth long and is kind, should dig the grave and help to bury all the malice and envy which at any time had intruded upon our peace and harmony.[10]

Jane was another expert on forgiveness, her knowledge hard-won. It's always our choice to allow charity to dig that grave and forgiveness to bury the evils of the past. Jane's story, and the examples we've seen of Church members who've chosen to forgive, show us two main things that are true: Jesus makes forgiving and healing and improving all possible, and forgiving doesn't have to mean forgetting. Often, we must remember.

---

10. Jane H. Neyman, "Be Forbearing and Forgiving," in *At the Pulpit: 185 Years of Discourses by Latter-day Saint Women*, ed. Jennifer Reeder and Kate Holbrook (Salt Lake City: Church Historian's Press, 2017).

THE WEIGHT OF LEGACY

Elizabeth Hale Hammond's research and writing vastly improved outcomes for heart transplant patients. In fact, she was one of the pathologists who developed the heart transplant grading schema for the International Society of Heart and Lung Transplantation. But when she first began publishing her research in 1989, transplant experts around the world thought she was crazy, and they weren't shy in their disparagement.

Dr. Hammond, now a professor emeritus at the University of Utah School of Medicine, was convinced that antibodies were causing a form of heart transplant rejection. For any who have forgotten biology, antibodies are proteins that circulate in the blood as part of the immune system. Their job is to identify intruders such as bacteria, viruses, fungi, and parasites, bind to them, then bind to other entities in the blood that will neutralize the intruders. I'll come back to Dr. Hammond, but let's shift for a moment to discuss one of the broad implications of her story—that of legacy.

It's only human to become concerned about questions of legacy, but we can easily take it too far. By legacy, I mean everything our life's work gives to the future. Our legacy includes the concrete things we achieve and create, as well as the relationships, ideas, and memories that persist beyond our death in the minds of those who knew us. In this way, the reputation we hold during our life can affect the legacy that outlives us. Worries about our reputations—and about our future legacies—not only threaten the quality of whatever work we do in the world but can lead us to be consumed by jealousies. When we focus so much on ourselves, we become poor colleagues and inadequate mentors. When other people say something to undermine our credibility, whether what they say has any truth in it or not, an obsession with our own standing can make us feel crazy and can distract us from the work at hand. As a scholar, I have been tempted and tormented by these feelings myself. I have seen scholars whose work I particularly admire suffer the same. I've definitely seen this suffering in scholars whose work and character I don't admire. And we see these dynamics elsewhere—in politics, in business, in the arts. In this chapter I invite you to reflect on those aspects of reputation and legacy that you can control and consider how to make the most of those, and then be free from worry over all that you cannot control. When we strike this balance, we see that two things are true about the weight of legacy: preoccupation with the status of our future legacy makes our lives cramped and heavy; and at the same time, gentle work to improve others' lives, without undue concern for our own reputation, creates the valuable legacy we naturally desire. Our legacy is a weighty matter, but it must be held lightly.

When Dr. Hammond was first introducing her research, the other heart transplant experts focused exclusively on immune cells as relevant to transplant success. Dr. Hammond wasn't a mad scientist conceiving her theories in some cave of the research wilderness. At least ten years before her own investigation, some general researchers had identified antibodies as playing an important role in transplant success, but the heart-transplant detractors ignored those earlier results. Despite the public disparagement, Dr. Hammond continued with her research, which, to their great credit, both the University of Utah and Intermountain Healthcare continued to support. She continued because she knew that her results were accurate and that this work was important to make heart transplant surgeries a viable and less-risky treatment option.

Consider the ramifications of that. She reported that her ability to focus on others, on the value of the information to patients and their doctors, "helped to drive me onward in the face of public rejection of my ideas."[11]

As she continued with her research, Dr. Hammond learned that even in the absence of immune cells, patients' risk of dying was nine times higher when antibodies were present. Other groups eventually began to recognize and publish similar findings. At last, 22 years after her first publication on antibodies in heart transplants, the international cardiology community accepted and came to depend upon her results.

Public disparagement is a potent dissuader. Dr. Hammond had to make the faith in her mind and heart stronger than the fear; she had to believe that God would direct her as she worked with honesty and diligence. Her desire to help patients and their families had to be stronger than her desire to be accepted.[12] She had to keep her focus on the value of

---

11. Elizabeth Hale Hammond, email to Kate Holbrook, Oct. 1, 2020.
12. Elizabeth Hale Hammond, "Faith and My Life as a Medical Scientist," in *Every Needful Thing: Essays on the Mind and the Heart*, ed. Melissa Wei-Tsing Inouye and Kate Holbrook (Maxwell Institute and Deseret Book, 2022), 39–45.

her work, rather than the polish of her professional status. Because she was able to stand firm despite the temporary tarnishing of her reputation, Dr. Hammond's legacy will include these life-saving medical discoveries. When we are consumed with what our reputation says about us, we invite torment into our lives. When we focus instead on what we can do for others, we invite God, purpose, and meaningful achievement into our lives. These create legacy as a byproduct rather than the main goal.

Legacy

I have greatly enjoyed the terrific Conversations with Terryl Givens recordings, co-sponsored by the Faith Matters Foundation and the Maxwell Institute, in which Terryl interviews Latter-day Saints about the intersections of their intellectual work and their faith. As an intriguing way into the interviews, Terryl frequently asks guests what they thought would be printed in their obituaries, or what they would wish to see there. My husband, Samuel Brown, is a medical researcher, an intensive care physician, and a professor of medical ethics, who also writes books exploring Joseph Smith's theological contributions. When Terryl asked Sam about his obituary, Sam responded that he most wanted his obituary to report, "He died defending his family from a grizzly bear attack with his bare hands." When Terryl pushed for more, Sam added, "Professionally I think I would like to be known as a figure who forced us to reconsider how we deliver intensive care during a life-threatening illness." Sam's words revealed his yearning to be self-sacrificing and brave, his desire to be remembered, and his focus on helping other people.

One of Church members' favorite contemporary artists,

Brian Kershisnik, responded to Terryl's obituary question with more attention to character than to art: "I aspire actually more to being. I hope that I am to be a good human being rather than an artist. Obviously, you're talking to me here because of my profession, but I derive a lot of power ... in my art from a search to deepen myself as a human. I hope that shows up in my obituary."

The writer Margaret Blair Young realized as she achieved her professional dreams that her covenants and her embrace of God's will had become increasingly important measures for her moving forward. "When I finally became a published writer," she acknowledged, "I realized it wasn't that big of a deal ... that was when I started taking my covenants very, very seriously and asked God for something that would matter, that maybe I could use my talents, but it wouldn't just be so I could have a byline.... The name I most want to be called by is disciple."

Margaret's past collaborator and friend, Darius Gray, has dedicated himself to providing resources, such as the Genesis Group, to Black Church members and to preserving and sharing their history. In his conversation with Terryl, Darius managed to convey charity, gratitude, humility, and faith in a few well-chosen words for his potential obituary: "To those whom I've loved, I love you still. To those who have loved me, thank you. See you soon."

Most of the responses, including many I haven't mentioned, and including my own, reveal discomfort with the topic of legacy. As Latter-day Saints, we know we're not supposed to aspire to fame or glory, but we still want our lives and our work to have mattered. As Brian Kershisnik acknowledged, "Obviously, you're talking to me here because of my profession." My own response was, "I've written some books in Latter-day Saint women's history that I feel have been good contributions. I think I'll be remembered generally through favorite recipes that have come from me. I've decided that's maybe in some ways a richer and more lasting visceral experience that people will have of my having been on this earth."

While I told Terryl that I thought recipes would be at the center of my legacy, I still hope that all the writing I have done, and the mentoring and the friendship, will have meant something. I wouldn't—and couldn't—spend most days of my life writing history without caring about it. I care immensely. But with my answer, I was trying to convey two things. First, there is so much that we can't control about our legacies. Academic currents and topics of public interest change over time, and I can't control the way that my writing will be received in the future. Second, I wanted to emphasize the importance of work that is less public, less celebrated, and also exceedingly meaningful. This kind of person-to-person work goes deep and goes long, spanning and shaping generations in ways that works of academic history typically do not.

Caretakers

Historian Laurel Ulrich has been honored with a Bancroft Prize, a Pulitzer Prize, a MacArthur Fellowship, and a Guggenheim Fellowship for her attention to women doing daily, uncelebrated work and for her exceptionally high standards and thinking behind that focus. "The real drama is in the humdrum," she wrote. And she proved it throughout her career.[13] Laurel is famous for the saying "Well-behaved

---

13. Laurel Thatcher Ulrich, "Vertuous Women Found: New England Ministerial Literature, 1668–1735," *American Quarterly* 28, no. 1 (1976): 20–40;

women seldom make history." She used those words at the beginning of an essay about women whom historians had ignored. There are obvious reasons why historians have not celebrated these women: they have seldom led countries or troops into battle; they haven't, like Henry VIII, beheaded their marriage partners in an effort to get an heir of their same sex; they weren't delegates to the Constitutional Convention. For much of the discipline's history, historians were interested primarily in public power, drama, and influence.

At its heart, history is an attempt to figure out what happened, but in doing so, we also inevitably define what mattered. And as a historian I recognize that we often leave out contributions that mattered the most. A general authority, Elder J. Devn Cornish, observed that parents and Sunday School teachers have a much deeper impact on people than do the more well-known and celebrated general Church leaders.[14] He's right. Although my brother-in-law met my grandmother only once, he still remembers how my grandma made him feel loved, welcomed, and comforted. She did so for many others, too, including me, who lived with her. Have I adequately preserved this work of hers?

The way we interact with children also teaches them what is worthy of recognition. We demonstrate what matters to us in the way we perk up over certain topics and praise other people. When a dad is moved by a story of someone sacrificing for the common good, children learn that that is the way to impress Dad. When a mother is captivated by the phrasing in a child's writing, the child learns that writing

---

Sarah Pearsall and Kirsten Sword, "Laurel Thatcher Ulrich Biography," *General Meeting Booklet, 2010 AHA Annual Meeting*. https://www.historians.org/about-aha-and-membership/aha-history-and-archives/presidential-addresses/laurel-thatcher-ulrich/laurel-thatcher-ulrich-biography.

14. Personal communication during a meeting on Oct. 5, 2017.

well is the way to impress Mom. We all want people to be aware of our efforts. We want to be interviewed for podcasts, hear ourselves mentioned on the news, be the recipients of awards. Not all our desire to matter is bad. We want our lives to have mattered in God's eyes. We want to be useful. But if we serve only to gain approval, we are missing out. Acting out of love for others is a more pure, effective, and satisfying motivation. Changing that motivation can be as simple as thinking about it. If we catch ourselves thinking about how something will make us look, we can switch our thoughts to focus on how our actions will benefit someone else. The real value, as Dr. Ulrich taught, is in the seemingly humdrum work of teaching and nurturing. Even historians are beginning to recognize that.

Reputation

As teachers, parents, and mentors, then, we are caretakers of others' legacies. Our words strongly influence the meaning people attribute to others' lives. When we communicate our esteem for the person-to-person work of care and service, we encourage others to value that work in the lives of those who have gone before. In this way, we can secure the legacies of worthy women and men who might have otherwise been forgotten—just as Dr. Ulrich's work does.

When we understand that we are caretakers of other people's legacies, we also understand that other people will be the caretakers of our own. This knowledge in turn influences how we shape, and then release, our own reputations. Church culture conveys mixed messages about what to strive for. We're not supposed to want recognition, and that message comes through when people receive callings. We say things such as, "No one was more surprised than I" or "I spent a sleepless night on my knees." At the same time, we admire Church members who have prominent callings or professional success. When led to think about our legacies, as Terryl Givens asked us to do, most of us admit that we care about how we are remembered.

When I was in college, a friend introduced me to the work of author and motivational speaker Wayne Dyer, who taught me some important lessons, including the fact that you can't control your reputation. Dyer said, "Your reputation is in the hands of others. That's what the reputation is. You can't control that. The only thing you can control is your character."[15] Belgian fashion designer Diane von Furstenberg said something similar once in an interview, which was fascinating because clothing design is a field in which reputation is both vulnerable and vital for success. "You can lose everything," she said. "You can lose your job, you can lose your parents, you can lose your wealth, you can even lose your health, but you never will lose your character. . . . Your character is something that no one can ever take away."[16]

We cannot control the way our legacy is received, except indirectly through teaching and modeling the qualities that other people value. We do have some control over the quality of our work, whatever our work may be: we can organize and exert ourselves to produce our best effort. Beyond that, I think that Dyer and von Furstenberg are right, that character is one of the few things we can control. But perhaps it's not even quite right to say that we control our own character. I would suggest that to build character, we can put ourselves

---

15. Wayne W. Dyer, *Staying on the Path* (ReadHowYouWant.com, 2009), 7.
16. Diane von Furstenberg, "Mental Toughness," *Masterclass*, 2020 (timestamp 1:45) https://www.masterclass.com/classes/diane-von-furstenberg-teaches-building-a-fashion-brand.

in places that invite God into our presence; we inhabit those places when we act. When we serve, pray, read scripture, or attend church, we invite the Divine into our lives and souls where God improves our character.

Motivation

For many of us, the hunger for our life to matter can lead us astray, toward ends that don't matter at all. Some of us seek that meaning through power and money. For those of us whose careers don't come with large salaries, we might channel our disappointment about wealth into sneering at those who are rich. When I was in seventh grade, my geography teacher was exceedingly bitter about money. In fact, his bitterness was one of my most prominent memories of junior high. One minute my teacher would be talking about state exports, and the next he'd be criticizing, again, the "people who live on the hill." Back then in my hometown, people who lived on the hill tended to have more money. He's certainly not the only person who, in defense of a fragile sense of self, has said insensitive things about others, but his embarrassing example reminds me not to sneer. Self-protective defenses of our own worth can blind us to what really matters, no matter our salary.

Reflect on your own responses to settings that make you feel vulnerable. At work, do you focus more on providing helpful feedback and encouraging other people, whether they be colleagues, clients, patients, or customers, or on making yourself look good? How do you speak about other people behind their backs? How graciously do you take criticism? If you feel that your reputation is always on the line, consider handing that worry over to Jesus. He will protect you while you can focus on the greater good.

I once heard Elder David A. Bednar suggest that if we're

trying to develop Christlike qualities for the sole purpose of being seen as good people, our prayers for help might not yield much result. But if we're trying to develop them on others' behalf, then God will help us. When I heard him say that, I felt in my heart that it was true. And I remembered how Dr. Hammond was able to withstand ignorant criticism of her work because she was motivated by others' welfare. Elder Bednar's insight is crucial to understanding the dynamics of righteous legacy. If I pray, "please help me to prepare a good talk so that people will know I'm smart," that's a weak prayer. If I pray, "help me to include content in this talk that will provide direction to someone listening, comfort to someone else, and will help others to feel God's love," that's a better motive. And it's a much better deal for the divine beings responding to my prayers, because they get to help me and others all at the same time—although I don't believe they do the math that way. While God may not count the cost, it is nevertheless true that when I focus on improving myself in ways that really matter, many are lifted along with me.

Vanity

I interpret the story of Nehor in the Book of Mormon as an indictment of people who are obsessed with reputation. When we meet Nehor in Alma 1, he shows up as the antagonist of the chapter, and some of us might assume we are blameless in comparison with him. "We aren't like him," we think, "because he is physically strong and wears 'very costly apparel.'" But the same verse that tells us about Nehor's impressive physical attributes also mentions that he "began to be lifted up in the pride of his heart, and even began to establish the church after the manner of his preaching."[17]

17. Alma 1:6

So we don't get a pass after all. Vanity can rear up in each of our hearts, in different ways and different settings. And I know that some of *us* like to imagine the Church established after the manner of our preaching. How many times have we muttered internally about a boring or boneheaded sacrament meeting talk? How often have we felt a flush of complacency because our accomplishments fit easily into a gospel framework? Isn't that a kind of vanity? Isn't it a subtle way of imagining the Church after the manner of our own personal preaching? Nehor is more like us than we'd like to believe.

After Nehor became angry with a righteous elderly man named Gideon and killed him during an argument—I assume because he was losing the argument and wanted to save face—he was brought before Alma the judge. The first thing readers hear Alma mention to Nehor is not the horrific murder but the sin of priestcraft, which professor of history and religious studies Grant Hardy, in the beautiful Maxwell Institute edition of the Book of Mormon, astutely defines as "religious fraud to gain wealth or power."[18] Alma says that if priestcraft were enforced among the people, it would "prove their entire destruction."[19] In other words, Alma taught that if people commonly committed religious fraud to gain wealth or power, it would destroy their society. Nehor's priestcraft, enabled by his vanity-fueled public reputation for strength and wealth, was corrosive to the entire community.

Nehor received a death sentence for having killed Gideon. Just before what the book calls his "ignominious death," Nehor acknowledged that his teachings had been

---

18. Grant Hardy, *The Book of Mormon: Another Testament of Jesus Christ, Maxwell Institute Study Edition* (Provo, Utah; Salt Lake City: Neal A. Maxwell Institute, BYU Religious Studies Center, Deseret Book Company, 2018), 244.

19. Alma 1:12.

false. But his deathbed repentance didn't receive enough attention, or at least its effect was insufficient to undo the destructive precedents he set. The reputation of his popular, prideful preaching had taken on a life of its own. Priestcraft persisted because Nehor's followers "loved the vain things of the world, and they went forth preaching false doctrines; and this they did for the sake of riches and honor." In response to their teaching, many people left the church and criticized those who stayed.[20] The narrator of the story draws a contrast between the riches- and honor-obsessed Nehorites, and the members of the Church of God. These righteous followers kept the commandments, listened to the word of God, and worked hard. Righteous teachers did not think they were better than the listeners. No one wore extravagant clothing, and they used extra resources to clothe and feed the hungry and tend to those who were sick.[21] Among the several lessons of this sad tale, one stands out: an obsession with our personal reputation for strength, wealth, or popularity can be contagious, as Nehor's was among his followers. What we desire influences what other people desire. We can ask ourselves: what does my life's work influence other people to desire and to work for? Do I influence others to desire wealth, strength, beauty, and status, or to desire—and work for—the welfare and flourishing of all?

In *The Unsettling of America*, author and farmer Wendell Berry offers another model to help us understand legacy in constructive ways. In this model, Berry contrasts the exploiter with the nurturer.[22] Exploiters want to get the most

20. Alma 1:16–23.
21. Alma 1:29–32.
22. Wendell Berry, *The Unsettling of America: Culture & Agriculture* (Sierra Club Books, 1986), 7–13.

for themselves out of any given resource or relationship, regardless of how their behavior affects that resource or relationship. Nurturers are primarily concerned with the *health* of resources, relationships, and communities. Berry's focus was on land. He described exploiters getting all of the resources they could out of a piece of land, then moving on to another piece once that land was wrecked. In contrast, nurturers built a sustainable relationship between the land and the people who worked it, so both the land and the people stayed healthy.

This exploiter/nurturer model can illuminate Nehor's priestcraft. Nehor was an exploiter. He didn't care about others' relationship with God, the health of the church, or anyone's well-being. He cared about his own wealth and power. Alma, on the other hand, devoted himself to people's well-being, to their relationships with each other and with God, and to the long-term health of the church. This exploiter/nurturer pairing relates directly to vanity and the way we think about legacy. Obsession with status tempts us to exploitative behavior in both our interpersonal relationships and in our public and professional work. Concern with nurturing people past and present, on the other hand, leads us to more careful thinking, to honesty, to building concepts and relationships that will sustain others for a long time.

Advocacy

One aspect of nurturing is advocacy, by which I mean supporting a cause or a person. We can be advocates for others, but we also have an advocate, a reliable one. Working on behalf of others makes Jesus Christ *our* advocate. Many of us have grown up hearing the familiar teaching from King Benjamin's address, that "when ye are in the service of your fellow beings ye are only in the service of your God."[23] I think a related idea is also true. When we are in the service of our fellow beings, God will put himself in the service of our efforts. Jesus Christ will amplify our work, bless our weakness, and guide our gifts of service to their proper recipients.

The advocacy of Jesus is one of the great gifts any disciple can enjoy, and it manifests itself in our lives in a number of ways. I'll briefly mention three:

First, the advocacy of Jesus Christ improves the quality of our work and helps it accomplish the good in the world that it has the potential to accomplish. The prophet Moroni struggled with a crippling anxiety in the face of his responsibility to prepare the records that would become latter-day scripture, the Book of Mormon. He poured out his heart to the Lord, expressing his fear that his personal limitations and the consequent weakness of his work would frustrate God's desire to speak to readers of the book: "When we write we behold our weakness, and stumble because of the placing of our words; and I fear lest the Gentiles shall mock at our words."[24] The Lord calmed Moroni's fears by promising that his grace would be sufficient for the book to accomplish its intended purpose, even in its imperfection. Perhaps counterintuitively, the Lord promised to advocate for Moroni's work not by magically fixing Moroni's flaws, but by opening the hearts of readers to his work in its weakness: he would "give unto the Gentiles grace, that they might have charity" when they read the book.[25] Each time an open-hearted reader is touched by the Book of Mormon, Jesus Christ's promise to advocate for Moroni's work is fulfilled.

23. Mosiah 2:17.
24. Ether 12:25.
25. Ether 12:36.

Second, when we are hurting from a poor evaluation, a boss who doesn't understand us, or a colleague who is trying to tear us down, we can have faith that our work will still influence the collective understanding for good. We can hope for the happy ending that Dr. Hammond received after her years of diligence. But maybe it will turn out that a supervisor's negative review was justified, however painful it feels to admit that. We can be grateful because the review, if we let it, will help us to do better work in the future. As our advocate, Jesus Christ can comfort us from either the pain of being falsely accused or publicly wrong. He can turn our minds toward the legacy that truly matters, and away from the reputation that does not.

Third, Jesus's advocacy can guide us toward truth and solid evidence. I believe this is what the diligence of Dr. Hammond allowed her to do—to bring out truth. We experience this frequently where I work in the Church History Department: a dose of divine intervention gets the right sources on our desks or brings a conversation with someone that leads us to frame a sentence differently. Often it is the Spirit who acts on Jesus's behalf in these situations. Before his death, Jesus taught his disciples that, although he would no longer be physically present with them, "the Comforter, which is the Holy Ghost, whom the Father will send in my name, he shall teach you all things, and bring all things to your remembrance, whatsoever I have said unto you."[26] Whether the work is scholarly, like mine, or practical, personal, or political, it will be stronger when we are guided toward true fact, true action, and true love by the Holy Ghost.

Mark Staker, who works in the Historic Sites division

---

26. John 14:26.

at the Church History Department, had such an experience when he was working on the renovation of the priesthood restoration site in Pennsylvania; his experience models how he blends scholarly work with the Savior's advocacy. Mark developed additional love and admiration for Oliver Cowdery, Emma Smith, and Joseph Smith during the project. "I wanted the site to reflect in detail everything I could learn about them as individuals, including their personalities, their sacrifices, and their contributions to the Restoration," he wrote. "I gave considerable attention to Oliver Cowdery as scribe. He walked all the way from Manchester, New York, through the snow and rain to meet Joseph. He arrived with his feet exposed in worn shoes and his toes slightly injured through the freezing. Right after he arrived in Harmony, he stayed up late into the night with Joseph as the two talked. Then Oliver took his meager school-teacher's salary and made the first payment on Joseph Smith's property both as a desire to help and as a sign of his commitment. He then immediately began to work as Joseph's scribe."

Mark thought a lot about what tools Cowdery would have used in his work as scribe. He studied the vast collection of nineteenth-century writing materials at Old Sturbridge Village, a site that recreates life in 1830s Massachusetts. He looked at inkwells, pen knives, and original quill pens found tucked between the pages of an old financial ledger or in the drawer of an old desk. He also discussed with scholars who'd carefully studied the original Book of Mormon manuscript how it had been produced. He learned that Cowdery's writing grew wider when the tip of his pen became old and flared out, and then his writing narrowed once more after starting with a new quill. Through this research, Mark determined that Cowdery would have used a turkey feather for his quill pens.

Mark looked for turkey feathers to put in the replica of the home where Joseph and Oliver had worked together, but he ran into a problem. He could buy an entire bag of goose feathers from China for $4.00, but turkey feathers came from American sellers charging $15 or $20 each, and he felt wrong spending that much money on them. So, he bought a bag of goose feathers and made over a hundred pens. Packing up a fistful of the goose quills, he took them along when he drove to Harmony to finalize the installation. But he knew the goose quills were wrong.

The morning of the opening, Mark arose before sunrise to put finishing touches on the home, including the quill pens. In his words:

> I arrived just as the morning light changed the home to a warm, rose glow. I was thinking about the feather at the time. I don't remember if I was praying for a solution, or if I was just lamenting not having one. There on the front stoop was a beautiful eleven-inch long feather from the tip of a wild turkey's wing.... I picked it up, pulled out a penknife, and then had the perfect quill sitting in Oliver's inkwell on the table a few minutes later.... I left part of the fletching on the pen so it would be clear what kind of bird had provided it.
>
> I'm grateful for that generous turkey. But in my mind it was God who orchestrated the experience. I think Oliver was pleased that his contributions to the Restoration were remembered and celebrated. I could say in my heart, "I know what you did." And he could whisper in my mind, "I know you know."[27]

---

27. Mark Staker email to Kate Holbrook, Nov. 2019.

To qualify for the kind of advocacy that both Mark Staker and Elizabeth Hale Hammond experienced, we have to let it in: believe in it, pray for it, and allow it to happen. An additional way we and they qualify is to keep working. "The Lord loves effort," as our prophet told a group of children in Palmyra, New York.[28] But perhaps the most important aspect of their qualification was that they were working on behalf of others—as nurturers, not as exploiters. They founded their legacy not on personal reputation, but on teaching and healing others.

Responsibility

The way we tell stories matters, and it matters in complicated ways for the legacies of the living and the dead.[29] The tradition of the Latter-day Saints attributes salvific qualities to history. Often Latter-day Saints think of history's saving qualities in terms of providing accurate records of events and as performing temple ordinances, seen as mandatory for salvation, on behalf of the dead. The first of these ordinances was baptism for the dead, which Joseph Smith initially introduced at the funeral of Seymour Brunson in August of 1840. Smith had worried about the fate of those who, like his brother Alvin, died without having been baptized. At Brunson's funeral he explained that Church members could be baptized by proxy for their dead ancestors, enabling their

---

28. Joy D. Jones, "An Especially Noble Calling," *Ensign,* May 2020, https://www.churchofjesuschrist.org/study/general-conference/2020/04/14jones?lang=eng.

29. This section was originally published in Kate Holbrook, "Saving History: The Perquisites and Perils," *To Be Learned is Good: Essays on Faith and Scholarship in Honor of Richard Lyman Bushman,* ed. J. Spencer Fluhman, Kathleen Flake, and Jed Woodworth (Provo, Utah: Neal A. Maxwell Institute, 2017), 81–92, at 87–89.

entrance into heaven.[30] This is one way the living save the dead.

Do the dead also save the living? Reflecting on baptism for the dead in his journal, Joseph Smith wrote, "For we without them, cannot be made perfect. Neither can they, without us, be made perfect."[31] When we study history, we give our ancestors the opportunity to save us as well—by helping us to feel and to know that we are not alone and by kindling our hope for the future. For the dead to save us, the living have an ethical responsibility to preserve and publish an accurate and inclusive range of their stories, and all of us have to read them.[32]

Our representations of those who came before is one of the ways we seek to honor the dead and remember their legacy. Historian Richard Bushman has remarked on this stewardship for historians: "Someday we will meet in heaven the people we write about, and when we do, we will have to look them in the eye and account for ourselves. Have we told their story as fairly as we know how? Have we told their story without distorting it in order to serve our own agendas?"[33]

Recently, I only narrowly avoided a grave error in the way I portrayed someone from the past. My colleague, Jennifer Reeder, and I compiled and edited *At the Pulpit: 185 Years of Discourses of Latter-day Saint Women*.[34] One of the

---

30. Matthew McBride, "Letters on Baptism for the Dead: D&C 127, 128," in *Revelation in Context: The Stories Behind the Sections of the Doctrine and Covenants,* ed. Matthew McBride and James Goldberg (Salt Lake City: The Church of Jesus Christ of Latter-day Saints, 2016), 273.

31. Joseph Smith, "Journal, December 1841–December 1842," 199.

32. Brett Rushforth, e-mail message to Kate Holbrook, Feb. 23, 2016.

33. Grant Wacker, "Reckoning with History: Richard Bushman, George Marsden, and the Art of Biography," Mormon History Association, Snowbird, Utah, June 11, 2016.

34. Jennifer Reeder and Kate Holbrook, eds., *At the Pulpit: 185 Years of*

talks is by Judy Brummer, a woman born and raised in South Africa who was the first adept Xhosa-speaking Latter-day Saint missionary. Brummer also produced early translations of portions of the Book of Mormon into Xhosa. When she arrived on her mission, she met a man named Goliat Kowa. Kowa had come across a Latter-day Saint pamphlet and based on it, founded a church among Black Africans that consisted of several congregations. He took Brummer and other missionaries to these congregations and taught his followers that they needed to be rebaptized, because he had not baptized them by the correct priesthood. This seemed to me a tremendous sacrifice. As is consonant with the churches Kowa and his followers would have known, church members provided a living for Kowa and his family. I find it astonishing that he so readily introduced members of his church to missionaries of the official Church of Jesus Christ of Latter-day Saints.

The only space I had to devote to Kowa was a brief footnote. I learned in doing research for that footnote that Kowa left the Church not long after the end of Brummer's mission. Turning to mission records, I read the report of an interview (not a transcript) in which Kowa was represented to have said there should be two churches, a White church and a Black church, and he was the prophet for the Black church. The report disclosed he had struggled with the idea that tithing should go to Church headquarters instead of helping to support his family (who scarcely had enough to eat). He purportedly said that he initially contacted President Kimball only because his church needed money, especially money for

---

Discourses by Latter-Day Saint Women (Salt Lake City: Church Historian's Press, 2017).

drums. And the congregations still did not have drums. This story felt a little incomplete to me, and it puzzled me. Why did he work with White church members for several years before voicing his philosophy about a Black church? Why would the man who so readily guided hundreds of believers from his church to the Church of Jesus Christ of Latter-day Saints suddenly leave over the issue of drums? Nonetheless, I wrote a brief footnote, which included his defection from the Church and his comment about being the Black prophet.

A few weeks later, I met with Judy Brummer to make sure one last time that I had the facts right in the introduction I had written for her talk. Although I felt dissatisfied with the Kowa footnote, in my mind I thought it was complete, and I did not plan to ask her about it. I had consulted the appropriate records. But while meeting with Brummer, my troubled feelings about that footnote increased, until I felt compelled to read it to her. Though she had completed her mission before the events reported in the footnote had taken place, she told me that there had been a personality conflict between Kowa and the American person keeping the mission record, the same person who had conducted the final interview with Kowa. She said she did not believe the translation between Kowa and his interviewer had been adequate, so the parties likely did not fully understand each other during their meeting. She told me that Kowa was an exceptionally spiritual and humble person. I still do not know what was actually said or intended in that significant interview with Bishop Kowa, just as the interview participants themselves might not. But I feel I have a more true sense of who Kowa was and how to represent him in a footnote; after I changed the footnote, my feelings about it were at rest.

This story I have just described is twenty-five times longer than the footnote. The footnote is a few sentences in a book that is several hundred pages long. I did not approach all of the footnotes with this degree of intense review. This particular footnote mattered because it was a representation of a life that is not otherwise extensively recorded. Despite the fact that I could not discover all of the details relevant to Kowa's later relationship to the Church, I felt I was spiritually guided to craft a representation of him that was truer to who he was. I have come to believe that a crucial aspect of our work as historians is to represent people in ways that are fair, meaning we consider the whole person and not just those aspects that help us to prove a favorite point. There is holiness and responsibility in the work of telling a person's story and preserving their legacy.

Sharing Legacy

Let's consider one additional aspect of legacy that we encounter even when we do good work for the right reasons, and we'll return to the Book of Mormon to explore this final point. As you have noticed, just because someone is in the scriptures doesn't mean that she or he did the right thing or that we should heed their words. Often, we have to figure out for ourselves whether what they have said or done is consistent with other Church teachings and with God's will. This dynamic is particularly obvious in the Hebrew Bible, where men sleep with their sons' widows and sacrifice their daughters, but it is at work throughout scripture which is, after all, human beings' attempt to record and make sense of their experience with the Divine.

In Alma 26, a missionary, Ammon, so exuberantly expresses the joy of having done good work on behalf of others and in partnership with God, that his brother softly accuses him, "Ammon, I fear that thy joy doth carry thee away unto boasting."³⁵ Ammon, Aaron, and their fellow missionaries had risked not just physical privations but their very lives in an effort to share information with the Lamanite peoples. As a result, thousands of Lamanites entered more deeply into God's love, experienced redemption, and exemplified integrity and charity in a way that then inspired and instructed the Nephites. Ammon had good reason to celebrate the legacy of what everyone together had accomplished—God, the Lamanite peoples, and the missionaries. Here is his response to his cautious brother's worry about boasting:

> I do not boast in my own strength, nor in my own wisdom; but behold, my joy is full, yea, my heart is brim with joy, and I will rejoice in my God. . . .
>
> I will not boast of myself, but I will boast of my God, for in his strength I can do all things; yea, behold, many mighty miracles we have wrought in this land, for which we will praise his name forever.
>
> He has brought [our Lamanite siblings] into his everlasting light, yea, into everlasting salvation; and they are encircled about with the matchless bounty of his love; yea, and we have been instruments in his hands of doing this great and marvelous work.³⁶

Ammon's exultations are worth our emulation because he focused on others' well-being and, while acknowledging the human effort involved, he still described their success as a gift from God. Ammon's words also teach us that celebrating legacy in humility and gratitude does not require that we

---

35. Alma 26:10.
36. Alma 26: 11–12, 15.

grovel. Ammon showed us how to feel good about helping others through gratitude rather than through boasting.

Terryl Givens's question about legacy has led us to a complex conversation. How we want to be remembered is an uncomfortable and potentially incriminating question, but it is also beneficial because it invites us to reflect. How better to avoid vanity than to examine our aims and to think through what we hope our lives will mean, so we can have a chance to make them mean something worthwhile? Maybe the Holy Ghost is right now inviting you to answer that question yourselves.

The legacy of the boy Joseph who sought, two hundred years ago, a quiet space to pray for spiritual direction is not in that boy's hands. His legacy lies now in our hands, in the ways we respond to the teachings and church structures he left behind. While he was alive, he created a worthy legacy by working for our salvation and *not* obsessing over his own reputation. He wanted others to have the forgiveness that was the first thing God offered him in the sacred grove. He wanted us to have the love of God in our lives and relationships that transcend the threats mortal life puts in their way. He worked as a nurturer, with faith, optimism, and strength.

I offer these thoughts in the spirit of empathy, encouragement, and also warning about the insidious vanity that leads us to care more about our own reputations than others' well-being. Our legacies do matter. The desire for our life's work to make a difference in the world, to persist in blessing our families and communities, is a worthy and righteous one. This is true. It is also true that a worthy concern for our legacy can bleed into a self-centered preoccupation with our status and reputation. Truest of all is this: lasting legacies are made through the quiet, gentle work of encouraging and remembering others, acting with integrity, and seeking truth through the Spirit. Securing our legacy need not become an exercise in boastful vanity. Instead, our efforts to make our lives matter can be interwoven, like the lattice top crust of an exemplary pie, with righteous motivation.

All travelers pass through a dark valley. We wonder whether our work matters, whether our dearest projects die with us, whether our efforts have failed. Let's have faith in God's abundance. Sister Michelle Craig taught at General Conference, "There may be times when you ... find yourself struggling to see how God is working in your life—times when *you* feel under siege—when the trials of mortality bring you to your knees. Wait and trust in God and in His timing, because you can trust His heart with all of yours."[37] God's abundance is the real antidote to the feelings that haunt us when we want our work to matter. With God in our hearts, we are more than enough.

The Legacy of Recipes

To honor Kate's desire for recipes to be the center of her legacy, we share her recipe for her favorite food: chocolate cake. More of Kate's recipes can be found at www.theawaycafe.com.

Every time someone asks, "What is your favorite food," I have the same answer: chocolate cake. I have known this about myself since grade school and, as a result, I have a lot of experience with chocolate cakes. This one is supernaturally good. One night, while I was getting ready for bed, the thought came to me that I should check the amount of cocoa powder in my favorite 9 x 13 chocolate cake and the amount of flour in my favorite Bundt cake (not chocolate), and if I would

---

37. Michelle D. Craig, "Eyes to See," *Ensign*, April 2020, https://www.churchofjesuschrist.org/study/general-conference/2020/10/14craig?lang=eng.

do those two things, I would know how to make the perfect chocolate Bundt cake.

When you take baking and chocolate cake as seriously as I do, you don't ignore that kind of a thought. I looked up the recipes, opened a new email to myself, and typed the ingredients the way I thought they should be. A few days later, when the family had a hankering for dessert, I made it. We all agreed that it was the best chocolate Bundt cake we'd ever eaten. On day one, the outside is crisp and the interior moist. On days two and three, the exterior becomes less crisp and the whole thing becomes more fudgy (though not actually fudgy). I had my cake expert friend make the recipe—she loved it. I made it for us again. Just perfect.

DOUBLE CHOCOLATE BUNDT CAKE

- ½ pound (two sticks) unsalted butter, room temperature
- 2 cups sugar
- 4 large eggs, room temperature
- 1 tablespoon vanilla
- 3 cups flour
- 1 teaspoon baking soda
- 1 teaspoon table salt
- 1 cup unsweetened cocoa powder, Dutch process, but natural also works
- 2 cups half-and-half, room temperature
- 2 cups bittersweet chocolate chips (my daughter likes 2 ½)

Heat oven to 325 degrees. Grease and flour a full-size Bundt pan (we like to use Baker's Joy spray for Bundt cakes—they always release well when we do).

Whisk together flour, soda, salt, and cocoa powder.

Cream the butter and sugar until light and fluffy, 4 to 5 minutes on medium with the paddle attachment of a KitchenAid mixer. Add the eggs one at a time, beating well after each. Add the vanilla and mix again.

With the mixer on low, add 1/3 of the flour mixture, then half of the half-and-half, then flour, then half-and-half, then flour. Scrape the bowl with a rubber spatula to make sure everything is well mixed. Then stir in the chocolate chips. This batter will really fill the pan. You might want to eat some of it, like I did today for my 4 pm snack, or bake a couple of cupcakes on the side (the cupcakes will be fully baked in maybe 22 minutes).

Pour into the prepared pan, smooth the top, and bake for 1 hour 25 minutes. (Do NOT overbake the cake. Our oven runs true to temperature, and we live 4000 feet above sea level, and this timing is perfect for us; 1 hour 27 minutes would definitely be too long). You may want to check your cake at 1 hour if your oven runs hot. A tester inserted into a melty chocolate chip may fool you that the cake isn't done when in fact it really is. Overbaked, this cake will be dry and the chocolate flavor dull (but it might still be the best chocolate Bundt cake you've eaten).

Cool in the pan for 10 minutes, then flip upside down onto a wire rack to cool. After it's cooled for at least 45 minutes, dust with powdered sugar to make it look even more appealing. The cake will still be warm, but no longer hot enough to melt the powdered sugar.

EPILOGUE

BY SAMUEL MORRIS BROWN

I spent a long August morning in Manhattan on the way home from Poughkeepsie, New York. I had just planted our second daughter (named for Sweden's patron saint) at her first year of college. I decided to wander the city, listening to a podcast, to clear my head. It was 9 a.m. on a Tuesday. Kate had breathed her last just before 1 a.m. that Saturday. I stepped onto the sidewalk, which smelled vaguely of wet sulfur and coffee grounds. I needed my body to do something other than grieve.

I loaded the Maxwell Institute podcast on my phone, wondering what the latest episode might be.[1] I lost my step when I saw her name on the screen: Kate Holbrook, PhD. The team had re-released her 2020 Neal A. Maxwell lecture, on legacy, in memoriam. I took a risk with my composure and pressed play. Her friend and colleague, Melissa Inouye, introduced her at length and with great care, and I remembered our early life together, when we were young enough to first be meeting Melissa in Boston. Then came that voice I

---

1. Kate Holbrook, "The Weight of Legacy," Neal A. Maxwell Lecture, Nov. 7, 2020, https://mi.byu.edu/maxwell2020/.

knew as well as my own, the voice I would never hear again from her mortal mouth. With that voice, Kate told a story that shook me with divine urgency: you matter because you love, not because you successfully compete. You are not your petty cruelty; you are your kindness. You can speak love to creation rather than dominion. As I strained in muddled sadness to know what would become of the balance of my life, I saw clearly that she had given that lecture in that forum so that I would hear it when I was drowning in grief as a newly widowing father. I'm not the first and won't be the last man to wander the streets of New York choking on tears. But she, now lost, had found me. She loved to share with me the poetry of e e cummings: we'd placed snippets on the tables at our wedding reception. "Nobody, not even the rain, has such small hands."[2] My dead beloved reached her small hands all the way to the center of me.

It wasn't until I read the essay version of her lecture, "The Weight of Legacy," in this book that I realized I had forgotten to mention her recipes in her obituary. She'd been clear about that imperative, and I'd blown it. Some old dogs really don't learn new tricks, however skilled and energetic the teacher. I know that she has forgiven me the oversight, as so many lapses before and after.

When did we first know she was dying? Not in the obvious sense that we are all dying. We'd always known that. Dying in the sense of too soon. There was the first tumor that tore the retina of her left eye, the tumor genomic profile that augured at least a 20% chance of fatal metastasis. The unrelated tumor in her skull a couple years later that

2. e e cummings. [somewhere i have never travelled gladly beyond], line 20, https://www.poetryfoundation.org/poems/153877/somewhere-i-have-never-travelledgladly-beyond.

EPILOGUE

left only the echoes of our anxiety and a titanium plate. The liver's glimmer on a CT scan followed by an MRI scan but lost for four months in the false reassurances of an oncologist who had lost his interest in clinical medicine and would soon leave it entirely. When that glimmer became a smudge, we guessed that we had one year left, maybe two. Then two became three, and we hoped that we might have five. We would be grateful for five; could there even be six? And then no more treatments would work. The tumors that oozed like toxic waste from her liver strangled her intestines, and she sputtered into smoky absence like a candle's flame leaning against a stiff wind.

With each milestone in the cascade of her advancing cancer, our shoulders sagged a little more under the weight of her impending death. There was so much she wanted to finish: books, articles, conferences, relationships, podcasts, events. And all this in forty hours per week because she fastidiously prioritized family, friends, our little ward family, the people she ministered to, and our neighbors.

As I think about her legacy now, in light of the urgent call of her Maxwell lecture, I see a legacy of blessing. After she died, our Jewish friends hoped in kind notes to us that her memory would be a blessing, like the names of Abraham and Sarah. I love that turn of phrase: "may her memory be a blessing," indeed. What she wrote, what she cooked, what she designed, arranged, and schemed were all blessings. They continue as blessings.

Kate had originally hoped to finish two books before she died: this book of essays for her beloved faith community and an adaptation of her dissertation, telling the stories of Latter-day Saint foodways in the twentieth century through the life of her grandmother, Belle Filmore Stewart. But dying of cancer was hard work, undertaken reluctantly. There was less time and energy than we expected to finish book projects. This collection of essays began as her attempt to fit as much as she could into life. She was invited to speak more often than she could accommodate. She tried to pick strategic opportunities that would allow her to write talks that could quickly become essays. She thus worked to be sure that the talks she gave grappled with the question of how two apparently contradictory things could both be true at once. She started with the theme of "two things are true." Each of these essays was born of that paradoxical insight.

Kate worried that we are too often brittle in this postmodern age of ours. We sometimes seem to swing from extreme to extreme without ever settling on the actual richness of life in Christ. In that richness, two seemingly contradictory things can both be true at the same time. The ever-wise Lisa Roper at Deseret Book noticed that although the alliterative rhyming of *two* and *true* was pleasant enough to the ears, the meaning was muddled. The point Kate wanted to make was that "both things are true." Lisa was right, and the new title stuck.

I've reflected on Kate's life and thought as long as I've known her: two-and-a-half decades so far. This reflection has come with special intensity over the last year of her mortal life and the first months after. As I have wondered with her, I've realized that what Kate was trying to explain with this concept of hers, that *both things are true*, was a model of Jesus Christ's Atonement.

We sometimes seem to think of Atonement as a "get out of jail" card, a divine voucher that settles a debt or pays off a bail bond. I honor those who feel strengthened by that image. And I believe that there's also much more to Atonement than the payment of a debt. At its core, Atonement is the bringing together of two things that are not in their nature wholly compatible: human and divine, heaven and earth, life and death, perfection and imperfection. Such apparently contradictory worlds come together in the person of Christ. This, to my eye, is the core gift of Jesus' Atonement. Both we humans and our divine parents can be one family; heaven and earth can be married in us. We imperfect people of dirt and mud can be perfect beings of light and spirit. These impossible possibilities are the lifeblood of Atonement. When I hear Kate saying that "both things are true," I hear her saying that, in Christ, apparent contraries are cast in faithful relation to each other. I hear in each one of these essays an attempt to trace the breadth and depth of Christ's Atonement.

There's another handful of moments relevant to this book that matter here. When chemotherapy was clearly no longer working, Kate and I thought we had six months, but instead we had three weeks. The manuscript wasn't quite finished, and Kate knew me well enough to know that my editorial hand was too heavy and foreign to hers. As we agonized about how to put the finishing touches on these essays, our friend Rosalynde Frandsen Welch felt an unusually strong inspiration to ask whether she could be of service in finishing any of Kate's writing projects. We wept as we saw the path to completion. Our friend Jana Riess shared her editorial skills as a labor of love. Miranda Wilcox exerted herself at the press, pulling in other writings to supplement and expand. And Kate's close friend and writing group companion for many years, Jenny Pulsipher, prayed her way through the last essay, the one that wasn't quite complete, wondering about how to stay true to Kate's voice in connecting the dots. And that gift of tongues came to Jenny. This coming together of strong and good women in love of our Kate—she of blessed memory—is as much the story of Atonement as anything else. We also express gratitude for the generosity of the reviewers as well as the expert copy-editing by Tessa Hauglid, interior design and type-setting by Kachergis Book Design, and cover design by Heather Ward.

I hope, and I believe that Kate would hope, that you will feel the sweet and life-giving breath of Christ in your lungs as you visit these essays, imagining how in Christ these contraries can be made one.

PUBLICATIONS OF KATE HOLBROOK

"Mapping Religious Diversity in Utah." Pluralism Project Archive, Harvard University, 2001. https://hwpi.harvard.edu/pluralismarchive/mapping-religious-diversity-utah-2001.

Edited with Ann S. Kim, Brian Palmer, Anna Portnoy. *Global Values 101: A Short Course.* Boston: Beacon Press, 2006.

"My Emergency Shelf." *Patheos*, May 16, 2012.

"Serving Community Members." *Patheos*, Sept. 17, 2012.

"Why I Pray. *Patheos*, Jan. 16, 2013.

"Weight, Weight, Don't Tell Me." *Patheos*, March 20, 2013.

"On Housework." *Patheos*, Sept. 26, 2013.

"A Song for the Body Electric." *Patheos*, Nov. 29, 2013.

"Scrap It: An Historian Contemplates her Imaginary Photo Albums." *Patheos*, Feb. 5, 2014.

"Primary Sources." *Patheos*, Aug. 13, 2014.

"Funeral Lessons from Emma Lou Thayne." *Patheos*, Dec. 13, 2014.

"Good to Eat: Culinary Priorities in the Nation of Islam and the Church of Jesus Christ of Latter-day Saints." In *Religion, Food, and Eating in North America,* edited by Benjamin Zeller, Marie Dallam, Reid Neilson and Nora L. Rubel, 195–213. New York: Columbia University Press, 2014.

"Radical food: Nation of Islam and Latter-day Saint Culinary Ideals (1930–1980)." PhD diss., Boston University, 2014. https://hdl.handle.net/2144/15142.

Co-authored with Samuel Morris Brown. "Embodiment and Sexuality in Mormon Thought." In *The Oxford Handbook of Mormonism*, edited by Terryl L. Givens and Philip L. Barlow, 292–306. New York: Oxford University Press, 2015.

Edited with Jill Mulvay Derr, Carol Cornwall Madsen, Kate Holbrook, and Matthew J. Grow. *The First Fifty Years of Relief Society: Key Documents in Latter-day Saint Women's History.* Salt Lake City: Church Historian's Press, 2016.

"Housework: The Problem That Does Have a Name." In *Out of Obscurity: Mormonism Since 1945*, edited by Patrick Q. Mason and John G. Turner, 198–213. New York: Oxford University Press, 2016.

"Lived Leadership." *Mormon Studies Review* 3 (2016): 30–36.

Edited with Matthew Bowman. *Women and Mormonism: Historical and Contemporary Perspectives.* Salt Lake City: University of Utah Press, 2016.

Edited with Jennifer Reeder. *At the Pulpit: 185 Years of Discourses by Latter-day Saint Women.* Salt Lake City: Church Historian's Press, 2017.

"Saving History: The Perquisites and Perils." In *To Be Learned is Good: Essays on Scholarship and Faith in Honor of Richard Lyman Bushman*, edited by J. Spencer Fluhman, Kathleen Flake, and Jed Woodworth, 81–92. Provo: Neal A. Maxwell Institute for Religious Scholarship, 2017.

"Living with Kids." *Design Mom.* 1 September 2021, https://designmom.com/living-with-kids-kate-holbrook/.

Edited with Melissa Wei-Tsing Inouye. *Every Needful Thing: Essays on the Life of the Mind and the Heart.* Provo and Salt Lake City: Neal A. Maxwell Institute for Religious Scholarship and Deseret Book, 2022.

SUBJECT INDEX

Accountability, xv, 99
Advocacy, 124–29
Ammon, 26, 133–35
Arrington, Leonard, 14, 20
Artistry, 37, 71, 114–15
Atonement, 33, 98, 142–44

Bahr, Kathleen Slaugh, 86–87
Beck, Julie, 65
Bednar, Elder David A., 60, 64, 120–21
Belonging, x, xv, 32, 80
Bigotry, 62
Brown, Samuel, 9, 25, 27, 47–48, 106, 114, 139
Brummer, Judy, 131–32
Burch, Alice Faulkner, 87
Bushman, Richard, 130

Cancer, x, 24, 49, 105–106, 141–42
Cannon, Martha Hughes, 83–84
Carruth, LaJean, 39
Character, 65, 112, 115, 119–20
Charity, 33, 35, 48, 86, 98, 105, 109, 115, 125, 134
Chocolate cake, 136–37
Jesus Christ, xiv–xv, 17, 32–35, 41, 45, 48, 50, 53, 69, 73, 75–77, 79–80, 82–83, 87, 94–95, 97, 99, 102, 107, 109, 120–21, 124–26, 131–32, 142–44
Church History Department, x, 3, 12, 39, 43, 69, 126–27, 151
Contraries, xii, 143–44
Courage, xv, 71

Covenant, 31, 48, 115
Covenant life, xii
Crucible, xiv, 75, 77, 82

Derr, Jill Mulvay, 12
Dew, Sheri, 65
Disciple, xv, 75–76, 83, 115, 125
Discipleship, xiv, 100
Discomfort, 18, 26, 32, 44, 115
Discouragement, 61, 75, 78
Dissertation, 11–13, 49, 141
Dissonance, 18, 32, 38
Divinity school, 10, 27, 151

Embodiment, 59
Empathy, 101, 135
Encouragement, 57, 135
Enos, 104–105
Eubank, Sharon, 53
Evidence, 40–42, 71, 75, 126
Exploitation, 77, 81, 123–24, 129

Faith, xii–xiv, 17–18, 20, 32, 35, 37, 44–45, 48, 50, 52, 54–55, 61, 64–65, 69, 75–76, 101, 113–15, 126, 135–36, 141
Faith crisis, 44
Fidelity, 45–47
First Vision, 51–53
Foodways, 35–36, 40, 141, 151
Forgiveness, xv, 23, 82–85, 95–100, 103, 105, 108–09, 135
Fruit, xvii, 46, 53, 58, 97

SUBJECT INDEX

Gardening, 90–91, 151
Gathering of Israel, xvii, 66, 68–69
Gender roles, 80
Givens, Terryl, 114, 119, 135
Grain storage, 35
Gratitude, 77, 82, 86–89, 115, 134–35
Gray, Darius, 102–03, 115
Guilt, 26, 55, 78, 105

Hammond, Elizabeth Hale, 111–14, 121, 126, 129
Healing, xv, 95, 98–99, 103, 109, 129
Heart transplant, 111–13
Heavenly Mother, 33
Hinckley, Gordon B., 55–56, 103
Historian, x–xvi, 3, 12,14, 26–27, 41, 52, 96, 101, 116–18, 130, 133
Historical method, xvi
Hoole, Daryl, 66
Holy Ghost, 56, 69, 126, 135
Hope, xii, 12, 35, 46, 65, 69, 71, 83
Housework, xiv, 75–91, 106

Injustice, xv
Inouye, Melissa, 139

Kallon, Mariama, 21
Kapp, Ardeth, 59–61
Kershisnik, Brian, 115
Kimball, Camilla, 55
Kimball, Spencer W., 54–56, 131

Lamanite, 104–05, 134
LDS Women Project, 3
Legacy, xv–xvi, 71, 75, 94, 111–14 116, 119, 121, 123–24, 126–130, 133–136, 139–41
Lenin, Vladimir, 93–94, 100
Living church, 31

Madsen, Carol, 14
Mary and Martha, 75, 80
Moroni, 96–97, 125
Mother Teresa, 63
Motivation, 118–20, 136

Nehor, 121–24
Nelson, Russell M., 7, 40, 54, 66
Neyman, Jane, 108
Nurturer, 61, 123–24, 129, 135

Oaks, Dallin H., 80
Only true church, 31–32
Ordinances, xiii, 34, 47, 53, 129

Perfectionism, 62–63, 77–78
Perspective, xvi, 16, 24, 26, 85, 98
Prejudice, 47, 103
Presentism, 102
Priestcraft, 122–24
Priesthood, xiii, 34, 37, 44, 51–56, 61, 70, 102, 127, 131

Racism, 87
Recipes, xiii–xvi, 11, 70, 73, 116, 136–37, 140
Recognition, 117–18
Reconciliation, 98
Reeder, Jennifer, 130
Relationship, 24, 26, 33, 35, 43, 45–49, 57, 64, 66, 82–87, 95–96, 107, 112, 124, 133, 135, 141
Relief Society, 14, 16, 35–36, 53, 57, 65, 67–68, 78, 84, 108
Remembering, xiii, xv, 4, 22, 38, 49, 54, 65–66, 75, 82, 86–87, 90, 93–95, 100, 102, 105, 107–09, 114, 117, 119, 121, 128, 130, 135, 139
Repent, xv, 66, 69, 101, 105, 123
Reputation, 112, 114, 118–19, 121–23, 126, 129, 135
Responsibility, xii, 55, 76, 81, 125, 129–30, 133
Responsible seeking, 41
Restoration, 33–34, 37, 54, 57, 127–28
Revelation, xiv–xv, 17, 33, 37, 41, 52, 67–69, 72–73, 80, 85, 102
    patterns of, 51
    process, xiv, 51, 53–54, 56–61
    receiving, 62–66, 70–71
Rogers, Aurelia Spencer, 57, 59
Russia, 6–10, 12, 21, 71, 93–94, 100

Scripture study, 24–25, 42, 64
Self-reliance, 35
Service, 45, 48–49, 63, 76, 118, 124–25, 143,
Smith, Joseph, xiii, 18, 37, 46, 51–52, 67–68, 73, 85, 114, 127, 129–30
Snow, Eliza R., 57, 68
Spiritual practice, 14, 37
Staker, Mark, 126, 129
Storehouse, 36, 43, 50

The Responsible Woman (James Christensen), 71–72
Truth, xiii–xiv, 32, 34–50, 62, 77, 97, 99, 102, 112, 126, 135

Ulrich, Laurel Thatcher, 116, 118,

Vanity, 121–22, 124, 135–36

Weil, Simone, 62
Wheat, 35–37, 41, 43, 50
Willis, Julie, 42–43

Young Women (organization), 48, 59–61
Young, Brigham, 35, 38–41, 84
Young, Margaret Blair, 115

Zion, x, xvii, 46

SCRIPTURE INDEX

Isaiah 43:25, 99
Jeremiah 31:34, 99
Joel 2:22–23, xvii
Matthew 6:19, 21, 88
Matthew 7:15–20, 46
Luke 9:46–48, 83
Hebrews 10:17, 99
Title page, Book of Mormon, 97
1 Nephi 22:24–25, 68
1 Nephi 22:28, 69
2 Nephi 2:23, 26, 97, 98
2 Nephi 31:20, 64
Enos 1:11, 13, 105
Enos 1:20, 22, 104
Mosiah 2:17, 125

Alma 1:6, 121
Alma 1:12, 122
Alma 1:16–23, 123
Alma 1:29–32, 123
Alma 26:10, 134
Alma 26:11–12, 15, 134
Ether 12:25, 125
Ether 12:36, 125
Mormon 8:12, 97
D&C 1:30, 31
D&C 44:6, 46
D&C 64:10, 85
Moses 4:23–24, 86
Moses 7:41, 13
13th article of faith, 37